ISLAND OF ISIS

*To speak of the dead
is to make them live
again*

ISLAND OF ISIS

PHILAE, TEMPLE OF THE NILE

WILLIAM MACQUITTY

Photographs by
William and Betty MacQuitty

Charles Scribner's Sons · New York

Acknowledgments

I wish to thank Mr T. G. H. James, Keeper of Egyptian Antiquities, British Museum, who most kindly wrote the Foreword and checked my manuscript. He also wrote the account of the part played by the Bankes obelisk from Philae in the story of the decipherment of the hieroglyphs. In the organizing and mounting of the outstandingly successful Tutankhamun Exhibition in London in 1972, which raised vast sums of money towards the saving of Philae, Mr James supervised the packing and transport of the priceless treasures before and after the Exhibition.

I owe special thanks to my many friends in Egypt; my deepest gratitude to H. E. Dr Abd el-Qadir, Deputy Prime Minister and Minister of Information and Culture, H. E. Dr Gamal ed-Din Mukhtar, Under-Secretary of State in charge of the Antiquities Service, and Dr Henry Riad, formerly Chief Keeper of the Cairo Museum. Warm thanks are due to H. E. Adel Taher, Under-Secretary of State in the Ministry of Tourism, and to the many members of his department who helped me in my travels. Lastly I would like to express my appreciation to the people of Egypt who were invariably helpful and courteous.

For Professor John Charnley and his colleagues at the Wrightington Hip Centre, Wigan, Lancashire, where this book was written and where the author received freedom to walk again.

Technical data

Cameras:	Two Nikon F2. One Nikkormat EL.
Lenses:	Nikkor Auto 20 mm F/3.5, 35 mm F/1.4, Micro Nikkor 55 mm F/3.5, Zoom Nikkor 80–200 mm F/4.5. All with lens hoods and filters.
Film stock:	Kodachrome II and TRI-X given normal exposure at meter readings.
Flash:	Three lightweight Mecablitz with mains charging units.

Designed and picture-edited by Craig Dodd

1 3 5 7 9 11 13 15 17 19 I/C 20 18 16 14 12 10 8 6 4 2

Printed in Great Britain
Library of Congress Catalog Card Number 76–5574
ISBN 0-684-14649-5

CONTENTS

Foreword by T. G. H. James, Keeper of Egyptian Antiquities,
British Museum, London   7

Chapter 1   Temples of the Nile   *13*

Chapter 2   The Worship of Isis   *49*

Chapter 3   The Ptolemies   *91*

Chapter 4   Philae   *119*

Chapter 5   The Fate of Philae   *155*

The Philae obelisk in the decipherment of hieroglyphics:
by T. G. H. James   *177*

Abu Simbel – Project Completed   *181*

List of the Ptolemies   *183*

Chronological table   *184*

List of principal gods and goddesses of Ancient Egypt   *186*

Further reading   *190*

Index   *191*

FOREWORD

It does not often happen that a calamity is reversed, especially in the fields of archaeology and the environment. A barrow ploughed flat by a careless or rapacious farmer can never be reconstituted; a country house demolished for redevelopment cannot be restored to what it once was, even if it is lovingly rebuilt according to its ancient form; a countryside ruined by an industrial complex or a motorway can never be quite the same again. Yet a distinction can be made between the destruction of the man-made and the devastation of a landscape; the former may be thought irrevocable, the latter a change which time will repair. Nature will not restore precisely, but she has the power to rehabilitate, to wipe out the rapacities of man, to replace what has been lost with something perhaps even better.

When plans were drawn up at the end of the nineteenth century to build a great barrage across the Nile at Aswan, it became apparent to the world of archaeology that a very large part of the archaeological inheritance of ancient Egypt in Nubia was threatened with destruction. The sites of towns, settlements and cemeteries were in greatest danger, particularly as most of them were unexcavated and many had never been satisfactorily identified. The creation of a great artificial lake behind the Aswan dam would flood these anciently occupied areas and wipe out for ever what still remained; mud-brick walls will not resist prolonged soaking. As for the stone-built monuments, concern was not at that time so very great, because most of them would re-emerge from the waters for some months every year when the river level lowered during the period of the Nile flood. An exception, however, was the island of Philae with its complex of temples set among palm trees. The setting was romantic, the antiquities evocative. Archaeologists were shocked at the idea of having these important monuments under water for most of the year. Romantic travellers were appalled at the prospect of the loss of the most famous beauty spot in Egypt.

Left: The goddess Hathor carved deeply into the sandstone of the right tower of the first Great Pylon at Philae. The sun's disc is held between her cow horns.

7

Amelia B. Edwards, a Victorian novelist, amateur Egyptologist and part-founder of the Egypt Exploration Society
(which flourishes today as strongly as ever), wrote lovingly
of Philae in 1877:

> It is one of the world's famous landscapes, and it deserves its
> fame. Every sketcher sketches it; every traveller describes it.
> Yet it is just one of those places of which the objective and
> subjective features are so equally balanced that it bears put-
> ting neither into words nor colours. The sketcher must perforce
> leave out the atmosphere of association which informs his
> subject; and the writer's description is at best no better than
> a *catalogue raisonnée*.

Such was the loss when the Aswan dam was built. For
many people Egypt would never be the same again. Philae
had been the climax to a winter's visit to Egypt for so many
travellers. And lost it was; for although Egyptologists never
forgot the temples, the setting and the landscape were gone.
For the visitor to Egypt Philae became a name only, not, in
general, a place to visit. With the construction of the great
new dam south of Aswan, new troubles for Philae emerged.
According to the new situation Philae lay between the old
and the new dams, partly submerged in the intervening lake
and subjected to constant fluctuations in the water level. In
a relatively short time this ebb and flow of the water would
wreck the scenes and inscriptions on the temple walls, and in
due course bring the structures down.

Right: Wall painting from the tomb of Nebamun at Luxor, showing him hunting marsh birds with a throwing stick while his wife and daughter collect lotus blooms.

In this book William MacQuitty tells the story of Philae's
place in history and of the imaginative way in which Philae
is to be saved. It is not a story of expectation which may
never come to pass. Work is already well advanced towards
the removal of the Philae temples to the island of Agilkia at a
higher level above the water. It will not be long before
visitors may once again take a boat across the lake and step
ashore on the substitute holy island. For some years, no
doubt, there will remain a strong feeling of artificiality about
the new site. But nature will intervene, trees will grow, the
marks of heavy engineering will be obliterated. And the
temples will in fact be the real temples of Philae. There
seems a very good chance that once again Philae may become
the climax of the Egyptian visit. This will be the bonus to be
enjoyed by the many thousands of visitors who will journey
to Egypt every year. It is a bonus over and above the archaeological rescue of a very important complex of monuments,
for which Egyptologists and the world at large have to thank

Overleaf: Nubian shepherds stand in the shade of an acacia tree whilst behind them the Nile thunders through its Second Cataract.

8

UNESCO. After Abu Simbel comes Philae. What is all the fuss about? Why so much money for such a project? Those who will come and see rescued Philae in future years will know at least part of the answer.

Most people who visited the Tutankhamun Exhibition in the British Museum in 1972 were perhaps only dimly aware that the proceeds from this exhibition in all places where it was held were to go towards the UNESCO fund for preserving the temples of Philae. They may have been rather more aware of the splendid photographs of Philae which lined part of their route as they trailed towards the entrance of the Museum in the never-ending queue. These photographs were generously provided by William MacQuitty, and they formed a valuable part of the 'stage-setting' which prepared

the visitors for the dramatic experience which lay before them.

His particular interest in the site of Philae, and in the problems of its rehabilitation, springing from his passion for the land of Egypt, its people and its monuments, has now brought Mr MacQuitty to the production of this handsome volume. The story of Ptolemaic Egypt is not one that is familiar even to those people who profess an interest in ancient Egypt. But it is a story of great fascination, in its intrigues and scandals more akin to Renaissance Italy than to Pharaonic Egypt. It provides the background against which the buildings on the island of Philae arose. The illustrations which enrich the text are, in many cases, of little-known monuments. They evoke a strange period in the history of ancient Egypt, and reveal an architecture and art which, while recalling ancient Egypt, are peculiar to the Graeco-Roman period. This book should do much to familiarize general readers with this period and help them to appreciate the particular virtues of its monuments. It also celebrates the rebirth of Philae, the 'Pearl of Egypt'.

T. G. H. JAMES,
Keeper of Egyptian Antiquities
British Museum

CHAPTER ONE
TEMPLES OF THE NILE

Herodotus rightly said that Egypt is the gift of the Nile. To later generations Philae was its pearl. It was along the banks of this river that the greatest of ancient civilizations was born, and it is therefore perhaps appropriate to begin the story of Philae at the beginning.

Some hundred and fifty million years ago the sea flooded a large part of Egypt, laying down enormous deposits of sand and the skeletons of innumerable tiny sea creatures over the underlying crust of crystalline rock and granite. Under the terrific pressures involved the skeletons became limestone and the grains of sand consolidated into the sandstone of which Philae is built. Much later, in the Pliocene period ten million years ago, the Nile Valley, already formed, was flooded once more by the rising level of the ocean which transformed it into a long narrow sea gulf reaching as far south as Philae. Into this gulf the river continued to pour silt and debris which gradually pushed back the sea until in the Pleistocene age, one million years ago, the sea was finally repulsed and the river once again began to erode its bed. Here, as it cut down through the layers of deposits, it left a record of the past.

In those days Egypt was humid, with lush vegetation and an abundance of animal life. Gradually the climate changed, and only the Nile remained to supply water to the parched land. Without this immense flood all would have become desert. As it is, only a narrow strip a few miles wide is available for cultivation, and sometimes this is reduced to a few hundred yards. Contemporaneous with the civilization of the Nile, three other civilizations were also stirring – those of the Sumerians in the valleys of the Tigris and Euphrates, the peoples of the Indus valley, and the Chinese on the Yellow River – but none reached the level achieved by the Ancient Egyptians or affected Western civilization to the same degree. For thousands of years the banks of the Nile were occupied by people who in spite of endless immigrations, conquests

Overleaf: Sugar cane farmers of Kom Ombo bring their crop to the Nile where it will be transported by sailing barges to the processing factory.

and natural disasters maintained an individuality of character which is exceptional.

In the prehistoric period Palaeolithic man ranged over the whole area of North Africa, but in the late Palaeolithic period 40,000 years ago, when pastures became desert, man withdrew from his old hunting-grounds to the neighbourhood of the Nile where traces of more settled occupation have been found. Positive evidence of cultivation comes in the Neolithic period 7,000 years ago when the inhabitants of the Faiyum and the Delta lived in settled agricultural communities growing cereals and flax, making linen, baskets and crude pottery. At El-Badari in Middle Egypt the earliest copper objects were found as well as many different shapes of fine pottery. Flint, ivory, bone and stone were worked with great skill and palettes of slate for eye-paint were first found in Badarian graves.

Perhaps the simplest way of discovering Egypt is to follow the Nile from its source to the sea. The river is 4,145 miles long but its most impressive feature is its final enduring flow through 1,700 miles of desert, where one would expect it to be swallowed up in the hot sand, to disappear for ever. On either bank the precious water is carefully fed to growing

Below: A boy herds cattle – c. 1400 B.C. wall-painting from the tomb of Nebamun at Luxor.

crops; the husbandry required to do this necessitated organization and an intricate system of irrigation which enforced an early discipline on the people. The source of the river always aroused intense curiosity; in about 450 B.C. Herodotus ascended as far as Philae. The Ptolemies sought its source and the Emperor Nero sent two centurions with an expedition which was blocked by swamps in Nubia and returned unsuccessfully. It was not until 1772 that James Bruce traced the beginning of the Blue Nile, and in 1852 the source of the White Nile was discovered by John Hanning Speke and Lt.-Col. J. A. Grant. The White Nile, or Bahr el-Abiad, has two separate water systems. One, the Albertine system, is fed by water from the Ruenzori mountains, one of the wettest places on earth with an annual rainfall of two hundred inches – enough to keep the river flowing all the year round even when the Blue Nile, which is fed by seasonal monsoons, has dried up. The second White Nile source is the Victoria system, which takes its water from the Mufumbiro mountains.

Below: Yoked oxen pull a wooden plough as they did in the days when these Great Pyramids at Giza were built.

The two systems of the White Nile meet in Lake Albert and continue their journey together as the Albert Nile, 3,600 miles from their final destination. Before reaching Khartoum

the river's progress is barred by the Sudd, a swamp of matted vegetation covering 50,000 square miles. This is made up of elephant grass, water hyacinths, bamboo, lotus-like lilies (the sign of Upper Egypt), and papyrus (the symbol of Lower Egypt), from which the Ancient Egyptians made their first paper. The thick mass filters the mud and debris from the water and gives the name Clear or White Nile to the river. The Sudd is so dense in places that it can support animal life, and even elephants can cross the firmer areas. Water buck, antelope, hippos, crocodiles, herons, cormorants, Nile geese and hawks, together with multitudes of mosquitoes, tsetse flies and flying insects, make up the varied population of the area. Many of these creatures were eventually worshipped in Ancient Egypt.

Whilst the White Nile moves in stately flow to Khartoum, its partner, the Blue Nile, or Bahr el-Azrek, descends in a tumultuous uproar from the thousand square miles of Lake Tana 5,800 feet above sea level. At the Tisiat Falls it thunders in a white downpour to the gorge far below, leaving a perpetual mist hanging over the scene. The river, now gathering speed, tears a gash through the country which, by the time it reaches Central Ethiopia, forms a gorge a mile deep and in

Below: Force-feeding of geese, a scene from a mural of the Sixth Dynasty at Saqqara (c. 2300 B.C.).

places fifteen miles wide. It is the debris from this vast erosion that is deposited as fertile silt in Egypt and its presence in the water gives the name Dark or Blue Nile. No human life appears on the steep rocky banks until 470 miles later when the river approaches the Sudanese border, nearly 5,000 feet below its starting point. Here Christian Ethiopian villages appear which gradually give way to pagan Negro settlements as the river continues through the ancient kingdom of Sennar, in the heart of Moslem Sudan. The river now grows steadily wider and warmer as it advances at a slower pace into the desert to join the White Nile at Khartoum.

The real strength of the two rivers lies in the Blue Nile. It provides six-sevenths of the total volume of water during the six months when it descends from the Ethiopian mountains like a tidal wave. By June the force of the flood is so great that the White Nile is forced back upon itself, while the Blue Nile rushes past carrying hundreds of thousands of tons of silt to Egypt. In January the tremendous rush subsides and the two rivers flow quietly side by side. For some miles there is a distinct dividing line between them, the White Nile showing light grey and the Blue Nile bluish green. Gradually they mingle into the milky green which gives its name to the

Below: Scene of fishing with a net and hooks from the tomb of Kagemni at Saqqara, Sixth Dynasty (c. 2340 B.C.).

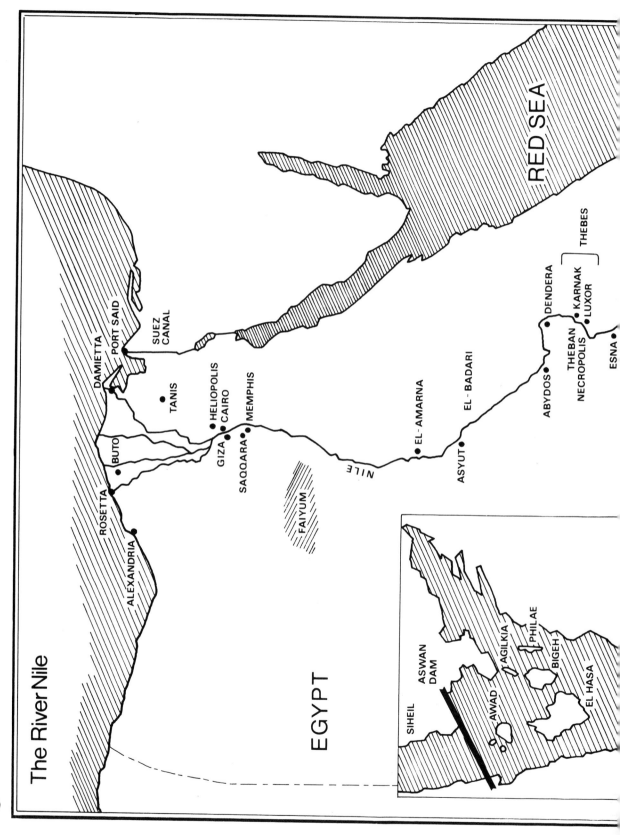

The River Nile

RED SEA

SUEZ CANAL

PORT SAID

DAMIETTA

TANIS

HELIOPOLIS
CAIRO
MEMPHIS

GIZA
SAQQARA

BUTO

ROSETTA

ALEXANDRIA

FAIYUM

NILE

EL - AMARNA

ASYUT

EL - BADARI

ABYDOS

DENDERA

THEBAN
NECROPOLIS

KARNAK
LUXOR

THEBES

ESNA

EGYPT

SIHEIL

ASWAN
DAM

AWAD

AGILKIA

PHILAE

BIGEH

EL HASA

20

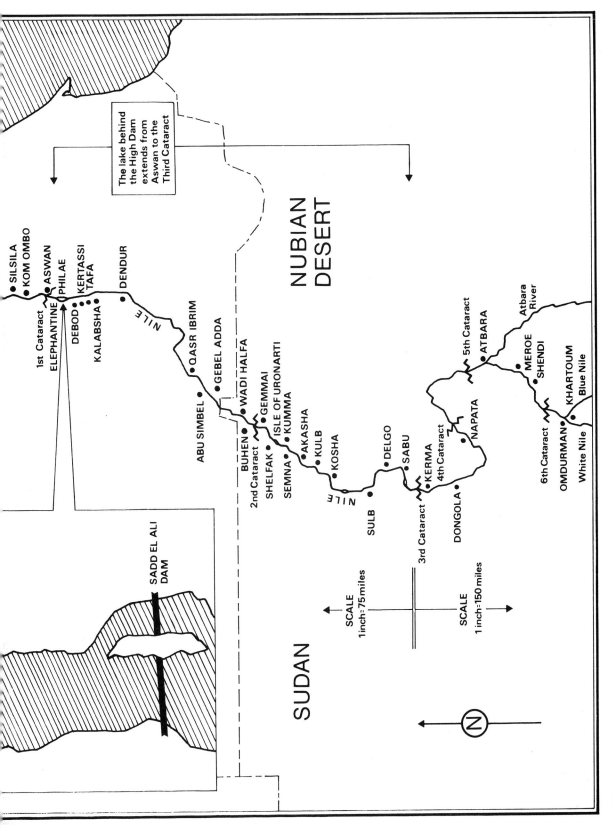

The lake behind the High Dam extends from Aswan to the Third Cataract

NUBIAN DESERT

SILSILA
KOM OMBO
ASWAN
PHILAE
KERTASSI
TAFA
DENDUR
DEBOD
KALABSHA
ELEPHANTINE
1st Cataract
NILE
QASR IBRIM
GEBEL ADDA
WADI HALFA
ABU SIMBEL
BUHEN
2nd Cataract
SHELFAK
SEMNA
GEMMAI
ISLE OF URONARTI
KUMMA
AKASHA
KULB
KOSHA
SULB
DELGO
SABU
KERMA
3rd Cataract
DONGOLA
NILE
4th Cataract
NAPATA
5th Cataract
ATBARA
Atbara River
MEROE
SHENDI
KHARTOUM
Blue Nile
6th Cataract
OMDURMAN
White Nile

SADD EL ALI DAM

SUDAN

SCALE
1 inch = 75 miles

SCALE
1 inch = 150 miles

N

21

colour 'eau de nil'. The river still has 1,750 miles to travel before it reaches the sea but it will have sustenance from one more tributary, the Atbara, another gift from the Lake Tana Highlands, before it flows into regions where there is no rainfall at all but only endless desert.

In this arid region where there is nothing to relieve the monotony and isolation we come surprisingly to the first evidence of the ancient civilizations; these are in sharp contrast to the lush but primitive conditions which have so far appeared on the banks. One hundred and eighty miles downstream from Khartoum near Shendi, between the Sixth and Fifth Cataracts, stand some two hundred ruined pyramids of Meroe, ancient capital and burial place of the Ethiopian kings whose first capital was Napata near the Fourth Cataract. They were devoted to the service of the god Amun and when unrest in Egypt gave them the opportunity they marched into the country and set up the Ethiopian Dynasty which lasted from 750 to 656 B.C. Under this Twenty-fifth Dynasty a revival occurred in the cultural and artistic life of Egypt, and much was done to restore the temples and establish the worship of Amun. Taharqa (689– 664 B.C.), the fourth king of the Dynasty, had the distinction of building the earliest monument now standing at Philae, a granite altar dedicated to Amun. The river continues past forts and monuments left by the invading conquerors, who came up the Nile in search of slaves, gold, ivory, spices and all the wealth of strange animals and plants that the country possessed.

Below: As a token of submission Nubians bring gifts of wild animals, ivory and slaves to their Egyptian rulers: temple of Ramesses II at Beit el-Wali.

At this point it is interesting to recall the following description of an exotic Abyssinian caravan from Amelia Edwards's book, *A Thousand Miles up the Nile,* an account of a journey she made during a visit in the winter of 1873–74. She travelled in a hundred-foot wooden sailing boat, or *dahabeeyah,* appropriately named the 'Philae', and her vivid eye-witness account provides a record of the country more than a quarter of a century before the building of the first Aswan Dam:

> I shall not soon forget an Abyssinian caravan that we met one day just coming out from Mahatta. It consisted of seventy camels laden with elephant tusks. The tusks, which were about fourteen feet in length, were packed in half-dozens and sewn up in buffalo hides. Each camel was slung with two loads, one at either side of the hump. There must have been about 840 tusks in all. Beside each shambling beast strode a bare-footed Nubian. Following these, on the back of a gigantic camel, came a hunting leopard in a wooden cage and a wild cat in a basket. Last of all marched a coal-black Abyssinian nearly seven feet in height, magnificently shawled and turbaned, with a huge scimetar dangling by his side, and in his belt a pair of enormous inlaid seventeenth-century pistols, such as would have become the holsters of Prince Rupert. This elaborate warrior represented the guard of the caravan. The hunting leopard and the wild cat were for Prince Hassan, the third son of the Viceroy. The ivory was for exportation. Anything more picturesque than this procession, with the dust driving before it in clouds, and the children following it out of the village, it would be difficult to conceive. One longed for Gerôme to paint it on the spot.

At Kerma just before the Third Cataract are the tombs of Egyptian governors of the Twelfth Dynasty. They are quite different from the tombs in Egypt, being low circular mounds containing the remains of great funerary feasts in which over a thousand oxen were slaughtered. The dead governor was laid to rest in a vaulted chamber in the centre and the door closed. Some three hundred Nubians, men, women and children, either strangled or stupefied with drugs, were laid in the corridor leading to the central chamber with a few personal belongings at their sides – pots, trinkets, weapons. Earth was piled over them making a funeral mound nearly ninety yards in diameter and ten yards high. This burial of the living with the dead was totally against Egyptian practice, but no doubt the inhabitants were following local custom for the burial of a great man.

All along the Nile between the Third and Second Cataracts were chains of strongholds – Sabu, Delgo, Sulb, Akasha, Semna, Kumma, Uronarti, Shelfak and Gemmai – garrisoned by the Egyptians to protect their trade routes. Each was within signalling distance of its neighbour and able to protect caravans or fleets in their passage. The garrisons were comparatively small, consisting of perhaps one to three hundred men. In case of a major revolt of the 'wretched Kush' (in Ethiopia) against their conquerors, the commander would signal down the long line of forts till his message for help could be sent on by swift galleys to Aswan. Meanwhile the garrison would defend the fort until the relieving force arrived. The great fortress of Buhen was the last of the chain which dominated the region and from here the message would be passed to galleys below the Second Cataract. It was a massive stronghold, the walls being eight yards thick and protected by a ditch cut out of the solid rock six yards wide and four yards deep. Just beyond the Second Cataract

Above: Tombs cut into the sandstone hillside opposite Aswan at Quebet el Hawa.

24

the once-flourishing border town of Wadi Halfa, like the ancient forts, has also been swallowed up in the rising waters of the Nile. Between the Second and First Cataract the river has submerged the Nubian villages and temples, monuments and forts, cemeteries and Christian remains. Happily many of the more important monuments have been rescued. Among the more famous of these are Buhen, Abu Simbel, Dendur, Kalabsha, Tafa, Kertassi and Debod. The last three temples now lie in orderly rows on the island of Elephantine awaiting the moment for their re-erection. Alas, the villages have been lost for ever. The Nubians have been resettled, many of them around Kom Ombo, far away from their whitewashed houses so beautifully decorated with vivid paintings of birds, flowers, animals, boats and even aeroplanes. The new homes stretch in orderly lines amongst fertile land, well-watered and safe from the vagaries of the river. In time the new generations will forget the past and merge into the Egyptian way of life.

The last temple before reaching the High Dam is Kalabsha. It is approached through a pass known as the Gate of Kalabsha where the dark granite rocks come close to the river on either side. On one of these rocks is an inscription stating that Isis, the goddess of Philae, owns the country for thirty *schoinoi,* some two hundred miles, stretching between the First and Second Cataracts. The temple of Kalabsha was restored by the Ptolemies and rebuilt by Augustus with subsequent additions by Caligula and Trajan. It is dedicated to the Nubian god Mandulis, but many Egyptian deities were also worshipped, including Amen-Re, Osiris, Isis and Horus. It is well-preserved and has been meticulously re-erected on high ground above the flood.

The concern of the world for the preservation of these ancient treasures and the active measures taken through the good offices of UNESCO for their rescue is something in which the nations involved can take unselfish credit. Politics, creed, colour and race have been forgotten in the current united endeavour to save Philae. The cost of this latest operation in UNESCO's Nubian campaign was originally estimated at $13,700,000, of which the Egyptian government pledged one-third. The Tutankhamun Exhibition, organized by the British Museum, raised some £650,000 for the project in London alone.

Philae itself is an island situated at the beginning of the First Cataract, from which the river descends on its way to the sea. Amelia Edwards described the descent of her boat in 25

1874 – there can have been little change in method since the days of the earliest Pharaohs:

The Sheykh of the Cataract is our captain, and his men are our sailors today; Reïs Hassan and the crew having only to sit still and look on. The Shellalees, meanwhile, row swiftly and steadily. Already the river seems to be running faster than usual; already the current feels stronger under our keel. And now, suddenly, there is sparkle and foam on the surface yonder – there are rocks ahead; rocks to right and left; eddies everywhere. The Sheykh lays down his pipe, kicks off his shoes, and goes himself to the prow. His second in command is stationed at the top of the stairs leading to the upper deck. Six men take the tiller. The rowers are reinforced, and sit two to each oar.

In the midst of these preparations, when everybody looks grave, and even the Arabs are silent, we all at once find ourselves at the mouth of a long and narrow strait – a kind of ravine between two walls of rock – through which, at a steep incline, there rushes a roaring mass of waters. The whole Nile, in fact, seems to be thundering in wild waves down that terrible channel.

It seems, at first sight, impossible that any Dahabeeyah should venture that way and not be dashed to pieces. Neither does there seem room for boat and oars to pass. The Sheykh, however, gives the word – his second echoes it – the men at the helm obey. They put the Dahabeeyah straight at that monster mill-race. For one breathless second we seem to tremble on the edge of the fall. Then the 'Philae' plunges in headlong!

We see the whole boat slope down bodily under our feet. We feel the leap – the dead fall – the staggering rush forward. Instantly the waves are foaming and boiling up on all sides, flooding the lower deck, and covering the upper deck with spray. The men ship their oars, leaving all to helm and current; and, despite the hoarse tumult, we distinctly hear those oars scrape the rocks on either side.

Now the Sheykh, looking for the moment quite majestic, stands motionless with uplifted arm; for at the end of the pass there is a sharp turn to the right – as sharp as a street corner in a narrow London thoroughfare. Can the 'Philae', measuring 100 feet from stem to stern, ever round that angle in safety? Suddenly, the uplifted arm is waved – the Sheykh thunders 'Daffet!' (helm) – the men, steady and prompt, put the helm about – the boat, answering splendidly to the word of command, begins to turn before we are out of the rocks; then, shooting round the corner at exactly the right moment, comes out safe and sound, with only an oar broken!

Below: The face of this Nubian bears resemblance to the carved features of the statue of Ramesses the Great at Memphis (left).

27

Today a modern road skirts the Cataract and follows the crest of the first Aswan Dam, giving a splendid view of the Cataract and the island of Siheil where traders inscribed their names on the numerous rocks and boulders before continuing on their way to Central Africa, the 'Land of Ghosts'. On the west side of this island are the ruins of a temple built by Ptolemy IV, Philopator, in honour of the gods of the Cataract. Below Siheil lies the island of Elephantine, which marked the traditional border between Egypt and Nubia. It was an obvious strongpoint controlling the river and its rulers claimed the title 'Keeper of the Gate of the South'. Whilst Elephantine was the military, administrative and religious centre of the region, Aswan on the bank of the river was the trading town. There is a small temple to Isis in Aswan built by Ptolemies III and IV. Ptolemy III, Euergetes I, is depicted with his wife Berenice, who gave her name to a cluster of stars below the tail of the Plough, known as Coma Berenicis. The story is that while Euergetes was at war with Syria, Berenice vowed that if he were successful she would cut off her beautiful hair and dedicate it to the gods. The king was victorious and the queen fulfilled her vow, whereupon the court astronomer declared that this little group of stars should be called the Hair of Berenice.

The river now commences the final stage of its long journey. The fall from this point to the sea 700 miles away is only one foot in thirteen thousand and the flow takes some two weeks in September and five in May to reach the Delta.

Beyond Philae the other great temples of the Ptolemies (the last dynasty of the Pharaohs) appear in their appointed sites. Twenty-six miles below Aswan the double temple of Kom Ombo dominates a magnificent curve in the river. It is dedicated to the crocodile-god Sobk and the falcon-headed Haroeris, the Elder Horus. Each god is allocated exactly the same honour and accommodation and, in accordance with the custom of the time, provided with two other divinities to make up his triad or trinity. Sobk had more famous companions than Haroeris. These were the goddess Hathor and the moon-god Khons. Haroeris, the Elder Horus whose reputation was beyond reproach, was given two minor deities, Tasent-Nofret, a secondary form of Hathor, and Penebtaui, 'The Lord of the Two Lands'. The temple is divided down the middle with Sobk and his triad on the right or eastern side and Haroeris on the left. The work of building the temple commenced in the reigns of Ptolemy V, Epiphanes, and Ptolemy VI, Philometor, and continued with Ptolemy VIII,

Right: Sandstone quarries at Silsila supplied much of the stone for the building of the temples in Upper Egypt, including Philae. The central stelae are engraved with invocations to the Nile god.

Eurgetes II, and by the time of Ptolemy XII, Neos Dionysos, the body of the building was completed as far as the Great Hypostyle Hall except for the decoration.

Fifteen miles north of Kom Ombo lie the great sandstone quarries of Silsila from which the temples of the Ptolemies, including Philae, were built. Limestone had been in universal use until the rise of the Eighteenth Dynasty (*c.* 1567–1320 B.C.), when sandstone almost entirely superseded its rival; practically all the temples of Upper Egypt are of this material. Luxor, Karnak, El-Qurna, the Ramesseum, Medinet Habu, Deir el-Medina, Dendera, Esna, Edfu, Kom Ombo, Philae and the Nubian temples are all of sandstone, though limestone is also employed in some instances in small quantities. This change of material must have made the sandstone cliffs at Silsila one of the busiest places in Ancient Egypt. From the Eighteenth Dynasty until A.D. 200, when the building of the Romano-Egyptian temples ceased, the quarry was worked by probably the most skilful masons the world has ever known. Seventeen centuries later, in 1906, the quarries were re-opened to provide stone for the great barrage which stretches across the river at Esna.

A. E. P. Weigall, in his *Guide to the Antiquities of Upper Egypt* (1910), writes about the excellence of the work done in Silsila:

> The great quarries have not their like in the world; and both for their vast extent and on account of the care and perfection of workmanship displayed in the cutting of the stone, they are to be considered as being among the greatest monuments of human labour known. We have admired the temples and tombs of Egypt as examples of the skill of the architect and builder; in the reliefs and paintings we have observed with wonder the art of the sculptor and painter; and in the inscriptions of the great Pharaohs we have read of splendid wars and wise administrations. But here we have the enormous record of the skilful handiwork of the Egyptian labourers; and it has been well said that 'in comparison with this puissant and perfect quarrying our rough-and-ready blasting looks like the work of savages'.

The secret of this magnificent work did not lie in numbers but in the almost perfect organization and unlimited patience which enabled these first masons to cut and transport stones with what we would regard today as utterly inadequate tools and appliances. Lining the banks of the river are the remains of shrines and inscriptions left by the Pharaohs and their chief officials of the Eighteenth and Nineteenth Dynasties. This place held a special religious attraction for the Ancient Egyptians long before the precious stone was exploited for its building qualities.

Downstream, the next temple to appear is Edfu, which lies on the west bank half way between Aswan and Luxor. The ancient name of the town was Edbu, which means the 'Town of the Piercing' since it was here that the falcon-god Horus pierced his eternal enemy, Seth. The present building was begun in the tenth year of Ptolemy III, Euergetes I, in 237 B.C. The Ptolemies, who came from Greece and were the last rulers of ancient Egypt, sought favour with the Egyptians by restoring old sites and building new temples in the Egyptian style. They also put their inscriptions on older temples like Karnak and Luxor, a practice that was continued by the Romans. Edfu is the most complete example of what an Egyptian temple should be. The main building was finished in 212 B.C., the tenth year of Ptolemy IV, Philopator, but trouble in Upper Egypt interrupted the work and the building was not opened until 142 B.C. by Ptolemy VIII, Euergetes II. The Hypostyle Hall (with roof supported by pillars), together with the forecourt and pylons, was completed in

Right: A Nile deity carries offerings of water in the temple of Kom Ombo.

Below: The god Horus represented as a hawk in his temple at Edfu.

57 B.C. during the twenty-fifth year of Ptolemy XII, Neos Dionysos, better known as Ptolemy Auletes or Ptolemy the Flute Player. The temple is dedicated to Horus, and amongst the inscriptions are representations of the great festival voyages when the goddess Hathor of Dendera made her spectacular journey up-river to meet her consort Horus at Edfu. But the time of the Ptolemies was nearing its end. The temple was completed when Julius Caesar was setting out to conquer Britain and only a score of years before the deaths of Antony and Cleopatra brought Egypt under the rule of Rome.

On the west bank, thirty-six miles from Luxor, the Thebes of ancient history, is Esna, sacred to the god Khnum, the creator god, who shaped man on a potter's wheel. The main temple was built by the Ptolemies; it was probably begun in 181 B.C. under Ptolemy VI, Philometor, whose cartouche appears on the gateway in the west wall. The *pronaos,* or vestibule of the temple, was either built or first decorated under the Emperor Claudius (A.D. 41–54), whose cartouches were placed on the cornice outside. Vespasian continued the work and his name appears in the decorations of the ceiling. On the twenty-four columns supporting the ceiling appear the names of Domitian, Trajan and Hadrian. The walls were decorated during the reigns of Antoninus Pius and Marcus Aurelius and completed by Commodus, Severus, Caracalla and Geta. The last emperor mentioned is Decius, A.D. 250. The temple now lies below the level of the streets of the modern town which has risen on the ruins of earlier cities. Esna is the last temple of importance before the river reaches the magnificent remains of the ancient city of Thebes 136 miles north of Aswan.

To the ancient Egyptians Thebes was known by many names: 'The Mistress of Temples', 'The Mysterious City', 'The Thrones of Two Lands'. In Homer's day the name had already come into use. He wrote: 'By fertile stream where, in Egyptian Thebes, the heaps of precious ingots gleam, the hundred-gated Thebes, where twice ten score in martial state of valiant men with steeds and cars march through each massy gate.'

The Greeks also called Thebes 'Diospolis Magna'. The city came into prominence in the early Middle Kingdom when the local rulers were successful in re-uniting the whole of Egypt after the anarchy of the First Intermediate Period. Karnak was probably the centre of the area and was the largest and most powerful temple in Ancient Egypt. It covers an area of

Right: The Propylon or Formal Gate of Ptolemy III, Euergetes, at Karnak.

Overleaf left: The fore-court of Kalabsha temple near Aswan, now safely re-erected above the rising waters caused by the High Dam.

Overleaf right: One of the hundreds of inscriptions carved on the boulders of Siheil Island by travellers to the Land of Ghosts.

more than sixty acres and could easily accommodate ten European cathedrals. The sun-god Amun whose house it was possessed 81,000 slaves, 420,000 head of cattle, 83 ships, 65 cities and towns supplying an enormous annual income of gold, silver, copper and precious stones. Luxor, like Karnak, stands on the east bank of the river. It was built by King Amenhotep III of the Eighteenth Dynasty, whose reign marked the zenith of Egyptian wealth and prosperity. The temple was dedicated to Amen-Re, but when Akhenaten, the son of Amenhotep III, came to the throne he renounced the worship of Amen and had the name of the god obliterated wherever it occurred. Akhenaten introduced monotheism to Ancient Egypt and only one god was recognized during his reign, Aten the sun's disc. However, this was only accepted during his lifetime, and the next king, Tutankhamun, under pressure from the priests reversed the situation and the people joyfully returned to worshipping their familiar gods. Reliefs and inscriptions of Ptolemies III, IV, VIII and XII appear in the temple, and in the Thirtieth Dynasty (360–343 B.C.) Nectanebos, who built the first temple at Philae, added the south-eastern gate to the temple of Montu.

On the western bank opposite the temples for the living stands the vast necropolis of Thebes. Here lie the dead Pharaohs, their Queens and families, their nobles and ladies. In lavishly painted tombs and in carved and inscribed mortuary temples their way of life is shown. The paint looks as fresh as the day the ancient artists applied it to the plastered walls. Here are musicians, dancers, servant girls perfuming their mistresses, banquets with singing and drinking. Farmers sow seeds, harvest corn and herd cattle. Everywhere the dead are seen continuing their earthly occupations and worshipping the gods under the protection of Osiris and Anubis who guard the underworld.

Thirty-seven miles north of Thebes stands the great temple of Dendera. Legend says that it was here that the god Horus defeated the god Seth, whom he finally crushed in the desperate battle at Edfu. The goddess Hathor is the local goddess of Dendera; she is the goddess of maternal and family love, of beauty, light and joy. Her form is that of a woman, above whose head rises the sun's disc held between a pair of cow's horns. The present temple was begun about 125 B.C. and completed in A.D. 60. Cartouches of the Ptolemies are inscribed in the temple. Outside on the rear wall is a large relief of the last Ptolemy, Cleopatra with Caesarion, her son by Julius Caesar, worshipping Hathor,

36

Below: The Valley of the Kings at Luxor, showing the tomb of Tutankhamun in the foreground with that of Ramesses VI behind.

Overleaf left: One of the sixteen columns in the forecourt of the temple of Kom Ombo. It is a splendid reminder of the use of colour by the Ptolemies, similar to that which once adorned the temples of Philae but since removed by the annual submersions. Overleaf right: The eastern colonnade round the court of the temple of Horus at Edfu.

Horus and Isis. Farther on Cleopatra and Caesarion appear in bas-relief worshipping Hathor, Horus Behudet, Horsmataui, the child of Hathor and Horus of Edfu. The front of the temple has six Hathor-headed columns and on the screens between them are damaged reliefs of 'The Prince of Princes, Autocrator Tiberius Claudius Caesar', standing before the gods of Dendera. It was from here that Hathor in her ceremonial bark visited Horus at Edfu.

Sixty-three miles beyond Dendera lie the magnificent remains of Abydos. Here the Kings of the First and Second Dynasties were buried, a custom that ceased in the Third Dynasty when the practice of pyramid-building came into fashion. Abydos is the Greek name for Abodu, 'The Mound of the Osiris-Head Emblem'. The cult of Osiris originated in the Delta and legend tells that his head was buried in this

sacred place. By the Sixth Dynasty every devout Egyptian wished to be buried as close as possible to the tomb of the great god of the resurrection. With the rise of the Nineteenth Dynasty Abydos reached its peak of power and wealth. Seti I and Ramesses II devoted themselves to building great temples which were dedicated to Osiris, Isis and Horus, the presiding gods of Philae. The power of Osiris grew to influence the greater part of the religion of Egypt. He was the deified dead king and above all the great god of the underworld. Everyone who died believing in him was identified with him; to speak of 'Osiris' So-and-so was equivalent to our own phrase 'the late'.

The long journey from the mountains and lakes of the sources of the Nile now draws to an end. There is a stillness and sense of presence in these ancient buildings, which are left behind as the river flows through landscapes of palms with their harvest of golden dates, green stands of corn and sugar cane set against the pale mauve of the desert hills. Buffalo, oxen, camels and donkeys move with ageless rhythm turning water wheels, carrying bundles, treading out the corn on the threshing floor as they have done unchanged since the days of the Pharaohs. Here and there white egrets and herons feed in the pastures unmolested by the *fellahin* (farm workers) in their blue or white gowns, or *galabiyas*. Women in black helped by their colourfully dressed children fill baked clay water pots at the river's edge and file up the steep banks with effortless grace. Everywhere men are bringing water to their fields with counter-balanced scoops, lowering them into the Nile and pulling them up to spill the contents into irrigation channels. Where the banks are high two or three of these *shadufs* work in series.

Gradually the outskirts of Cairo appear, the largest city in Africa, whose five million inhabitants depend on the unfailing flow of the river for their existence. A hundred miles from the sea the Nile begins to fan out in canals and waterways into the green of the Delta, formed by the deposits of silt which push the land ever farther into the Mediterranean. Of the original seven mouths only two remain, one at Damietta and one at Rosetta, finding place of the famous Rosetta stone, the key to decipherment of the hieroglyphs – along with the obelisk at Philae – and prized possession of the British Museum. This, then, is the end of the river, a river which has exercised a unique influence on the story of civilization of the world. The overriding necessity for survival taught the Ancient Egyptians the arts of river engineer-

Right: The Nilometer on the island of Elephantine at Aswan. The gauge cut in the stone was used to measure the height of the inundation.

ing and land surveying. To calculate the dates of the arrival and departure of the inundation they were forced to study astronomy. The yearly overflow obliterated all landmarks and it was necessary to re-measure the land annually and to keep accurate registers of the area belonging to each owner. Above all it became an important duty of the rulers to impress the people with a strong sense of the rights of ownership. Every year there were fresh disputes about boundaries and these required the establishment of settled laws and the enforcing of judicial decisions. The Nile was also a controller of taxation. The higher the flood the greater the area of land irrigated and the larger the harvest and so, inevitably, the heavier the tax. The water level was recorded on Nilometers, one of which is still to be seen on the island of Elephantine and another on Philae.

Besides instilling law and order, taxes and measurement, the Nile offered an incomparable means of transport through inhospitable territory. The present boats on the Nile bear a strong resemblance to their ancient forebears, from the small fast *feluccas* with their tall single sail to the great two-masted sailing barges on which every type of cargo can be carried. Another great gift of nature to Egypt is the direction of the wind which usually blows from north to south so that it is 41

Below: The façade of the temple of the ram-god Khnum at Esna. City has been built upon city until the roof of the temple is now level with the present streets.

Right: Huge pillars in the Hypostyle Hall in the temple of Karnak carry the solid stone beams which supported the roof. The pillars were set close together as stone beams of more than a few yards were impracticable.

Left: Sunset at Esna.

possible to sail with the wind against the current to the south and to rely on the flow of the river when travelling north. This convenient waterway enabled engineers to bring the colossal monuments cut from the pink granite of the Aswan quarries as far as Memphis and Tanis, 600 miles away near the coast. Colossal obelisks and figures of the Pharaohs, some weighing a thousand tons, were dragged to the water's edge along specially-built ramps using relays of wooden rollers and pulled by hundreds of men. They were then carefully manoeuvred with ropes and levers onto huge barges for their long journeys.

Perhaps the greatest achievement of these people was their ability to remove huge stone masses in a single piece from the living rock with only the most primitive equipment, and then to produce carvings so fine in detail and finish that they equal the best work done today. Their method of work is clear, as several of these colossal pieces still rest in their original positions, only partly freed from the mother rock. The best example is an obelisk in the granite quarry at Aswan. Here, as in Philae, the underlying crystalline granite conveniently comes to the surface to offer itself to the masons. The enormous shaft lies on its side in the quarry, its

Below: An unfinished carving of an Osiris figure in the quarry at Aswan.

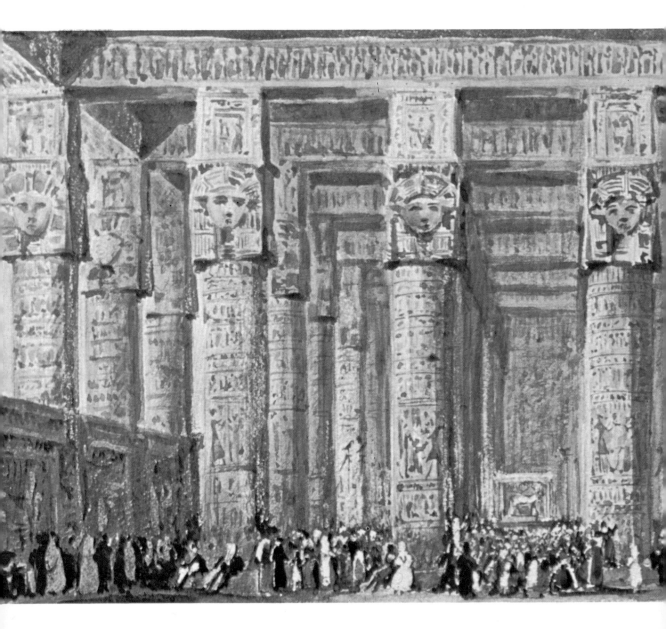

lower surface still part of the living rock. It is 137 feet long and the base is fourteen feet square, the estimated weight being 1168 tons. If completed it would have been the largest single block of stone handled in human history, though the colossal statues of Ramesses the Great at Tanis and the Ramesseum weighed close on a thousand tons each. Unfortunately as work progressed a flaw developed in the stone and the project had to be abandoned. The method used was to pound a trench round the outline of the obelisk with tough pieces of green dolerite. When the trench was wide enough for men to work in, it was increased in depth until the masons were able to undercut the base and cleave the huge stone from its bed. The only tools available, apart from the pounding rams, were copper and bronze chisels and saws. Once clear of its bed the obelisk was taken to its site, where it was first polished with dolerite dust and then meticulously carved. This enormous unfinished work is an everlasting testimony to the ability of the Ancient Egyptian masons as workers of stone.

Egyptian obelisks were monuments to the glorification of the Pharaohs and have always attracted worldwide admiration. Numerous examples of the smaller ones exist in museums, whilst the large ones are to be found in many capital cities. Rome has a great number crowned with incongruous crosses. There are two in England, one affectionately called Cleopatra's Needle, which does not belong to her but to Thutmosis III, and one from Philae which stands in the garden of Mr Ralph Bankes at Kingston Lacy in Dorset. America has the fellow of Cleopatra's Needle which graces Central Park, New York. There are two in Istanbul and four in France, of which the best known is in the centre of the Place de la Concorde, surrounded by the swirling traffic of Paris. This 78-foot stone was brought to France by Champollion and erected on 25 October 1836 in the presence of Louis Philippe, King of France, his Queen and a tumultuous crowd of nearly a quarter of a million citizens. It is the twin of the one that still adorns the temple of Luxor erected by Ramesses the Great in 1300 B.C.

The earliest history of Egypt is written in the strata of the rocks, but the Ancient Egyptians finally used those rocks to inscribe their way of life and their beliefs. Their earthly dwellings crumbled away, but their stone-built temples and tombs survive to tell their story.

CHAPTER TWO
THE WORSHIP OF ISIS

The worship of Isis at Philae was the culmination of the religion of Ancient Egypt. The Bible bears some similarity to the older cult in the description of the creation of the world. In the ninth century B.C. a prophet who lived in Judah wrote: 'God created heaven and earth. And the earth was without form, and void; and darkness was upon the face of the deep. And the Spirit of God moved upon the face of the waters.' The First Book of Moses, Genesis, continues in verse 7: 'And God made the firmament and divided the waters which were under the firmament from the waters which were above the firmament.' Two thousand years earlier the Ancient Egyptians believed that in the beginning there was nothing but a waste of darkness and chaos. From this emerged the sun-god Atum, who came into existence by himself and produced a god, Shu, and a goddess, Tfenet. Shu provided the air upon which all breathing creatures depend. Tfenet provided the water which surrounded the earth and upon which it floated; when a well was dug this water was struck. These two deities bore Geb, the earth, and Nut, the sky. Geb and Nut finally produced Osiris, Isis, Seth and Nephthys. The gods so created formed the divine company of nine, the Ennead which in later texts was regarded as a single divine entity. From this the Ancient Egyptians conceived the universe as represented by the figure of the air-god Shu standing and supporting with his hands the outstretched body of the sky-goddess Nut, with Geb the earth-god lying at his feet.

The religion of Ancient Egypt is extremely complex and our knowledge of it comparatively slight. It is probable that the earliest inhabitants were fetishists, worshippers of objects considered to have special properties – the stone or stick with which a dangerous animal had been killed, a tree that had given shelter, and so on. Historic religion starts with ancient hieroglyphs and inscriptions, statues, carvings and wall paintings which reveal the sun-god Atum and many 49 local deities, who, like the Christian saints, were especially popular in their own areas. In addition to the Ennead there were in earliest times universal deities subordinate to the sun-god but of considerable importance throughout all parts of the country. Among these were Hapi, god of the inundation, and Nun, god of the ocean.

Although the Nile was the obvious giver of life to the early men of Egypt it was not the great river and its precious waters that first stirred thoughts of worship in their primitive minds. It was the sun, relentless bearer of death, that they supplicated. Life and death were constantly in the thoughts of these pre-dynastic people and there were plenty of grim ·reminders. The all-pervading dryness preserved every dead creature until the living devoured it. The yellow sand of the desert swept relentlessly against the thin line of

Right: The sun-god Re flanked by Isis and Nephthys, in the tomb of Nefertari in the Valley of the Queens, Luxor.

Left: A Nile god showing the pendulant breast symbolizing the fruitful Nile.

green pasture watered by the Nile and swept over it the moment the river subsided. Of the two elements the sun was the more powerful, and man bowed before it. Sun worship was not confined to Ancient Egypt; the early Britons practised it at Stonehenge, and Incas and Aztecs made blood-thirsty sacrifices to propitiate their sun-god. The life-loving Ancient Egyptians omitted human sacrifice but worshipped the sun above all other gods. Each day it rose in the east, heralded by the chattering of dog-faced baboons, sacred watchers for the dawn, who from their treetop vantage points were first to see its glorious majesty rise above the horizon and announce to the world that all was well. Overhead the god rode in splendour across the clear Egyptian sky to vanish in a blaze of glory in the sunset of the western desert. At night it entered the underworld where all mankind go after death. Here it was carried in a heavenly bark through the waters of the underworld until it rose once more at dawn to make another triumphant voyage across the heavens. The sun and the moon were regarded as the eyes of Atum, creator of the world. In addition men worshipped living things. Animals, birds and reptiles were elevated to the position of gods, possibly because they had abilities that man had not. The bull was worshipped for its strength and the ram for its virility. Gazelles could outstrip man and birds could escape from him through the air. Crocodiles, hippopotamuses and snakes all had their special virtues.

In the first burials the dead were not mummified; the shallow graves in the hot dry sand allowed nature to dry out the corpse so efficiently that skin and hair have been preserved to this day. Around the body some household goods were laid, pottery, flints, weapons and the like, proof of belief in a hereafter. As these primitive men became more sophisticated their graves became more elaborate. The bodies were wrapped in matting and the graves lined with brick or wood. Unfortunately these attempts to preserve the body failed. They prevented contact with the dry absorbing sand and putrefaction set in, the corpse collapsing in natural decay. In their desire to preserve the body they had to experiment, and this led to elaborate forms of embalming.

Concentration on the problem of life after death brought into being a group of people who studied the sun and moon and the movements of the stars. These were the first astronomer priests and the precision of the movements of the heavenly bodies enabled them to plot the seasons accurately.
52 These men produced a culture which laid the foundations

Below: The beautifully wrapped mummy of an ibis removed from its protective jar.

for many aspects of our modern world. Their achievements are reflected in the fields of medicine, astrology, taxation, law, military strategy, writing, religion, poetry, painting, sculpture, drama, ritual, mathematics, agriculture, irrigation, ship building, the domestication of animals, the development of bows and arrows, nets and traps for hunting and fishing, and even the breeding of such birds as ibises for offering to the gods.

The ibis, through its identification with the god Thoth, the ibis-headed god of writing, became eventually the emblem of Imhotep, the chief official of King Djoser of the Third Dynasty. Imhotep was the designer of the first stone pyramid and is often thought of as the founder of medicine. He is presumed to be buried at Saqqara in the vicinity of his pyramid and excavations by the late Professor Bryan Emery on behalf of the Egypt Exploration Society have revealed a labyrinth of passages containing an estimated half-million mummified ibises. The birds are thought to have been offerings to Imhotep for healing the sick, who made pilgrimages to his tomb. Each ibis is beautifully wrapped in fine linen and sealed in an earthenware jar.

Below: Baked clay pots used to protect the mummified ibises before they were placed in the underground rooms and passages at Saqqara. Nearly half a million of these mummified birds have been found – it is thought that they were votive offerings to the deity.

The priests were also shrewd politicians and gained positions of enormous power by declaring the Pharaohs to be god-kings, which meant that the Pharaoh had to co-operate with the priests to rule the country. The only revolt against this supremacy of the priests occurred when Pharaoh Akhenaten rejected the multiplicity of gods and goddesses and decreed that there was only one god, manifested in the sun's disc, and that no other god should be worshipped. Akhenaten and his beautiful wife Nefertiti had a brief success with the new faith and even built a new city to their god, the 'City of the Horizon of the Sun's Disc' at El-Amarna. Here for some twelve years the new religion prospered, but after the death of Akhenaten the priests regained the upper hand. The court returned to Thebes and the new city decayed never to be reoccupied. The power of the priests was paramount.

Man had begun by worshipping the sun; later he grew to worship creatures which possessed qualities he could not match. But then he learnt fresh skills and with his bow and arrow, spears and throwing sticks, gained control over the animals, which he could kill or tame, and over the birds, which he could bring down with his arrows. Yet the Ancient Egyptians were a thrifty people, and gods, whether bulls, birds, crocodiles or cats, were not to be wasted. The priests united man and beast, a marriage of human intellect with animal capabilities. The form usually taken was to place the animal head on the human body. This was done so artistically that even today the composite result seems both natural and attractive. Sometimes various aspects of the god or goddess are depicted. Hathor, the goddess of love, drinking and all the delights of the senses, is shown as a beautiful woman with the ears of a cow or, again, with the horns of a cow holding the sun's disc between them. She is a special goddess in the temple of Philae where she is identified with Isis.

The god frequently had a wife and child, forming a triad which was worshipped in the same temple. The most famous of such trinities is the family formed by Osiris, Isis and their son Horus. Philae was one of their temples. The story of Osiris is the most important myth of Ancient Egypt. Even today fishing boats in the Mediterranean carry the eyes of his son Horus on their bows. In Malta, that most Christian of countries, the fishing boats wear them for protection against the dangers of the sea. The myth of Osiris is, according to Sir Alan Gardiner in *Egypt of the Pharaohs*, 'too remarkable

and occurs in too many divergent forms not to contain a

Below: Isis suckling her son Horus (from the Egypt Exploration dig at Saqqara).

Below: The god Seth, brother and murderer of Osiris.

considerable element of historic truth, though we must be on our guard against over-speculative reconstruction of details. Of the three chief actors involved the one whose nature and origin are least open to dispute is the god Seth, whom Greeks identified with their Typhon on account of his turbulent character.'

One popular version held that in antiquity Osiris ruled as King of Egypt in a humane manner, teaching men the rudiments of civilization and bringing prosperity to the country. His brother Seth was jealous of him and conspired to kill him. At a banquet he persuaded Osiris to enter a cunningly wrought chest, which Seth and his accomplices then closed and threw into the Nile. The river carried the chest down to the sea where it was washed ashore near the Phoenician city of Byblos. Meanwhile Isis, the distraught wife of Osiris, searched everywhere for her lost husband. At length she succeeded in discovering the chest which she took back to Egypt and there mourned over her husband in solitude. She then buried the body and went to see her son Horus, who was being brought up at Buto on the Nile. During her absence Seth, while engaged in a boar hunt, found the body and cut it up into fourteen pieces which he scattered throughout Egypt. As soon as Isis heard what had happened she set out to find the pieces. This she succeeded in doing and Re the sun-god sent down his son Anubis to wrap the body in bandages like those of a mummy. Isis beat her wings and caused breath to enter it and Osiris miraculously lived and moved again.

Osiris, unable to return as an earthly king, reigned in the spirit world as god of the dead. In this capacity he did not conflict with any of the established gods and no Egyptian, whatever his local god or goddess might be, had any difficulty in also adopting Osiris and his creed. This was essentially that man, after death, lived again in the underworld, provided the proper rites had been observed. Every Egyptian finally believed that because Osiris died and rose again to live in eternal blessedness he too could obtain the same destiny provided that the requirements of religion had been duly satisfied and that he became one with Osiris. Osiris was also regarded as being embodied in other roles. He was one of the Nile gods and with each inundation of the river he was believed to have risen again. He was also a god of fertility. Funeral trays carved in his shape were filled with earth and planted with corn which sprouted to life beside the mummy in the darkness of the tomb.

Isis was regarded as being the divine symbol of mother-hood; she was also a mourning goddess, one of the four goddesses who protected the dead body. During the last centuries of antiquity her great cult centre was her temple of Philae, where she was worshipped with her husband Osiris and their son Horus. Horus when he grew up was trans-formed into the falcon-headed god of the heavens and received the name of Re-Harakhty, 'the sun, the Horus who is on the horizon', in which form he was worshipped at Abu Simbel. Horus now set out to avenge his father's death, and after many terrible contests with Seth was at last victorious. Gods, however, could not be killed, so Seth was able to continue his existence in much the same way as Satan does.

Just as Osiris, after his death and revival, was judged to see if he were a fit person to receive eternal life so too would anyone be who wished to share his immortal state. In the great Hall of Justice the dead person had to appear before forty-two terrible beings. These were the assessors of Osiris, who had become the supreme judge.

In the Hall of Justice stood a large balance to weigh the heart of the deceased against truth, which was represented by a feather, the symbol of Maet, the goddess of truth. Some-times a statuette of the goddess herself, wearing an ostrich feather in her hair, was placed in the scale. Should the weighing go against the deceased a terrible creature, Amemit, composed of a crocodile, a leopard, and a hippopotamus, waited to devour him. The two scales of the balance are always shown in equilibrium, which is presumably the most favourable position for the dead person – the weight of the heart, the instigator of man's actions, being exactly equal to truth. Before each of these assessors the deceased had to state that he had not committed the sin for which that assessor had authority to punish. This statement is the famous 'Negative Confession' which embodies the moral code of the Ancient Egyptians. It consists of a series of denials such as: I have not killed; I have not spoken falsely; I have not given short measure; and so on. The deceased is finally led by Horus before his father Osiris.

Although there was a great multiplicity of gods and god-desses in Ancient Egypt and a considerable diversity of doctrine there was one belief that the whole population held in common, the firm conviction that the life of man did not end with death. Men, they were convinced, continued to live as they had on earth provided that the necessities for their existence were assured to them. It was, therefore,

Above: Bastet the cat-goddess, whose cult-centre was at Bubastis in the Delta area. She was a kindly deity and often wore a gold ring in her ear. The ancient Egyptians believed that the mummified cat, shown above right, would continue her life in the Underworld.

essential that the body should be carefully housed and protected from decay. There was a divine spark in men – they had been fashioned by the ram-god Khnum from clay, and life had been given to them by the god. It was unthinkable for these people with their intense enjoyment of living that all these pleasurable experiences should vanish with the advent of death. The preservation of the body was essential for eternal life. This was the most important consideration, for without a body there could be no survival after death. In addition to the body men were considered to have a 'Ba' and a 'Ka'. The 'Ba' resembled the western idea of a soul which lived on after death. It was originally conceived as a bird and later as a bird with a human head. It was believed that the spirit left the body at death and flew freely about, but could return to the body at will provided that it did not decay. The 'Ka' was presumed to be a kind of guardian double of the body which was born with it and which accompanied it through life to protect it. The 'Ka' did not expire with the body at death but continued to live and care for the deceased in the future world.

Right: Carving of the 'Ba' or bird-soul of a dead person, Kalabsha.

57

As we have seen the bodies of the pre-dynastic people were preserved by the drying effects of their shallow sand graves, more by accident than by design. The new concepts required that the bodies should be made incorruptible and this was eventually achieved by embalming. Several mummies embalmed by the methods described below were discovered at Philae and now repose in the museum at Aswan.

The earliest embalming consisted of soaking the body in salt solutions and tightly wrapping it in linen bandages. However, this failed to preserve the vital organs. Later the procedure became more sophisticated and was surrounded with ritual. A specified period of seventy days was required for completing the process and the results were almost permanent.

Embalming was a highly skilled profession, whose practitioners were a mixture of surgeon and priest. They first washed the body with water from the Nile; then, through a slit in the left side made with a flint knife, the organs were all removed except for the heart, which was required for the judgment weighing. The most vulnerable parts were separately mummified and placed in four canopic jars in a solution of natron and aromatic spices. The jars were then sealed with carved stoppers. Up to the end of the Eighteenth Dynasty these stoppers took the form of human heads, probably in the likeness of the dead person, those of Tutankhamun being particularly beautiful specimens of the art. After the Eighteenth Dynasty the heads of the four sons of Horus were used, possibly because they afforded greater protection. Each organ, besides having a son of Horus as a protective minor deity for the stopper, had guardian goddesses for the jars themselves. The stomach was protected by the jackal-headed Duamutef and the goddess Neith, the intestines by the falcon-headed Qebhsenuef and Selkis, the lungs by the ape-headed Hapi and Nephthys, and finally the liver by the human-headed Imsety and Isis the goddess of Philae. The brain was removed either through the nose by breaking the ethmoid bone or through the ear. The brain and body cavities were then washed out with palm wine, and other astringents such as cedar oil were used to dissolve out any residue. It is not clear if the kidneys were left in the body or what happened to the brain, but all the organs and materials were kept and buried in the vicinity of the tomb or in the tomb itself. It was essential that nothing should be lost that belonged to the body. The empty body cavities were now packed with natron, a naturally occurring compound of

Right: The eyes of Osiris watch over the dead in the tomb of Senedjem, Luxor.

58

sodium carbonate and sodium bicarbonate which dehydrated the body efficiently and acted in addition as a preservative.

The first half of the seventy days was allowed for drying the body, after which the cavities were packed with linen or other substances. Nile mud was occasionally used, in order to restore the dead person to a shape resembling life. The slit was sewn up and a patch of leather or other material bearing the eye of Horus, a powerful protective amulet, was placed over the stitching. (It was, incidentally, from Alexandria that Horus and Isis entered the legend that surrounded Buddha in Gandhara, in northern India, and thence travelled to China, where the goddess Isis resembled the Chinese Queen of Heaven, Kwan-Yin, who, like Isis, was also Queen of the Seas. In Japan she was called Kwannon. It is possible that there is some connection between the eyes on Chinese junks and those on the Mediterranean boats. In Ancient China the custom of preserving the dead amongst their possessions may also have been influenced by Egypt.)

In Ancient Egypt the final days of the embalming ritual were devoted to ensuring that the dead man would journey safely to the next world, thanks to the example of Osiris. As the ceremony advanced sacred amulets were placed on other parts of the body, the eye sockets were plugged with artificial eyes or wads of linen, and, most important of all, the heart scarab was placed on the breast. On the belly of the scarab was an exhortation to the heart not to act as a hostile witness against the deceased when it was in the balance in the Judgment Hall of Osiris. It is possible, therefore, that the heart, like the 'Ba', was also a free agent.

The most elaborate part of the embalmer's art was the exquisite bandaging of the mummy. This started with the extremities. Each finger and toe was separately wrapped and frequently encased with finger and toe stalls of gold or silver. The penis was wrapped in a state of erection. During the bandaging prayers from the Book of the Dead were read by the priests, and ointments, spices and resins were poured on the bandages. After the fingers, the forearms were bandaged, then the upper arms, which were folded across the chest and bound in position. Between the layers of bandages were placed a great variety of precious objects, rings, bracelets,

Overleaf: General view of the Book of the Dead of the Scribe Ani. His heart is being weighed in the balance against the feather of truth by Anubis while Thoth, the scribe of the gods, writes down the result. If unfavourable the fearsome Amemit, part crocodile, leopard and hippopotamus, waits to devour the deceased. Below: Mummified crocodiles at Kom Ombo where they were especially worshipped as the living form of the crocodile god Sobk, shown, right, with the goddess Hathor.

pendants, collars – a treasure chest which attracted robbers with such success that so far the only king's tomb with substantial funerary equipment known to have escaped pilfering was that of Tutankhamun.

When the bandaging was complete the body was wrapped in shrouds, and these were fastened with four transverse bands and three which ran from head to foot. The high priest pronounced the final benediction; 'You live again, you live again for ever, here you are young once more for ever.' The mummy was then placed in its Osiris-shaped coffin and taken to the tomb by the relatives, friends and officiating priests who stopped for prayers at a temple or temples on the way.

From earliest times the tombs of the Egyptians were provided with everything that was considered necessary for the after-life. At first this consisted of simple things used in the daily life of the period: pottery vessels, weapons, food and drink. Later, in the time of the Dynasties, the tombs of Pharaohs and nobles contained household furniture, clothing, jewellery, even chariots and thrones which they used whilst alive. In addition to these domestic goods there were religious and magical objects designed to assist the dead man in dealing with conditions in the underworld. These varied over the centuries but consisted in the main of magical texts and inscriptions either on the coffins themselves or written on papyrus and enclosed in the tomb. Magical amulets and charms of many kinds were put in the tomb, including un-

Below: The ceiling of the tomb of Seti I, showing the gods as part of a heavenly constellation.

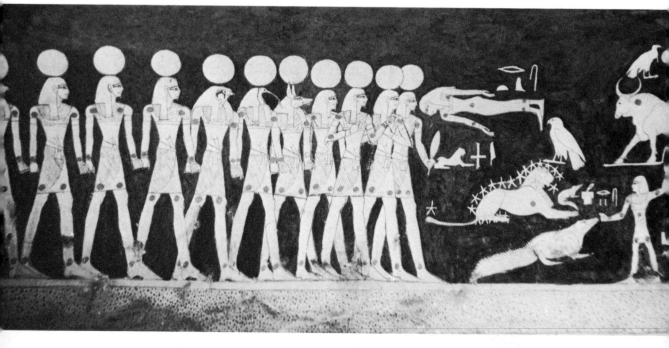

baked mud bricks suitably inscribed with texts from the Book of the Dead which were placed in niches in the four walls of the burial chamber to prevent the approach of enemies. Little figures and models of all sorts – of funerary boats, bakers, brewers, ploughmen and all the workers that would have been employed on the estate of the deceased – were placed beside the coffin. These models were substitutes for the scenes painted on the walls of earlier tombs and also included little Osiride statuettes called 'Ushabtis' or 'Answerers'.

The Egyptians believed that just as on earth there was ploughing and planting, harvesting and irrigating, so there would be in the underworld: and no one would be exempt from this work. It was possible, however, for the deceased like the living, to supply a deputy, and this took the form of the Ushabti. When his master was called, the Ushabti-figure would answer the call and work in his place. Chapter Six of the Book of the Dead says: 'O Ushabti! If I am detailed for any tasks, to cultivate the fields, to carry water, to take away sand to the east and to the west, then say thou, ''Here am I''.' There was always doubt in the Egyptian's mind as to whether the Ushabti might rebel or avoid his tasks, and to insure against this Ushabti-figures were provided for every day of the year. Later, as many as seven hundred were found in one tomb, divided into groups under the control of foremen carrying whips. Written on the wall was the warning:

Below: A blind harper sings his song in the tomb of Nakht: 'Spend a happy day and weary not thereof; Lo, none may take his goods with him, and none that hath gone may come again.'

Right: The crowning of a Ptolemy by Nekhbet and Buto at Kom Ombo.

'Obey only him who made thee,' a warning to the Ushabtis not to work for anyone else.

The Book of the Dead was a collection of religious and magical texts known to the Egyptians as the 'Chapters of Coming-forth by Day'. Its purpose was to secure for the deceased a satisfactory after-life and to enable him to leave his tomb when necessary. No copy of the work contains the complete text, but each one is adjusted to the particular needs of the person concerned or perhaps to the amount he could afford. The finest copies are beautifully illustrated with ritual scenes, including one of the deceased standing before his judges in the Great Hall of Justice. Many of these papyrus scrolls look as fresh as the day the scribes wrote them over three thousand years ago. Some copies were done in advance and left blank spaces for the name of the purchaser.

In the First and Second Dynasties the shallow graves in the desert sand were replaced for the kings and nobles by elaborate underground burial chambers, over which was raised a brick-and-earth rectangle called a *mastaba* because it was similar in shape to the benches found outside native houses. The burial chamber was surrounded by storerooms for the funerary goods, and the *mastaba* was supplied with false doors by which the dead man might leave and re-enter his eternal home. As time passed the tombs became more complex, possibly to afford better protection for the mummy. Djoser, the first king of the third Dynasty whose tomb was built at Saqqara by the famous Imhotep, was covered not by one *mastaba* but by several, piled one on top of the other, each one being smaller than its fellow and thus providing six steps, the topmost being two hundred feet high. The rect-angle formed by the first step measured 411 feet by 358 feet. Beneath this Step Pyramid lay the royal burial chamber sur-rounded by storerooms and passages leading to small burial chambers designed for members of the royal family.

The Step Pyramid was the forerunner of the true pyramid, the finest example of which is the Great Pyramid of Cheops, the second king of the fourth Dynasty. This is 755 feet square at the base, rising to a height of 481 feet, and is the sole survivor of the seven wonders of the world. Perhaps because of its size the position of the burial chamber was changed three times. First, it lay beneath the ground on which the pyramid stood; next, it was placed in the lower level of the pyramid itself; and finally, near the centre of the mass. This was thought perhaps to be the safest place for the huge granite sarcophagus containing the mummy of the Pharaoh,

Right: The famous Step Pyramid at Saqqara, the first stone-built building and forerunner of the Great Pyramids at Giza. Built by Imhotep for King Djoser, c. 2650 B.C.

but in spite of the fact that the whole pyramid was sheathed in fine white limestone and that no entrance could have been visible the sarcophagus no longer contains the body of Cheops, nor has it ever been traced. This tremendous undertaking shows not only the absolute power of the Pharaohs but also the reverence in which they were held by their people. The operation is estimated to have taken 100,000 men twenty-two years during which time they moved six million tons of stone to cover an area of thirteen acres. The stones would have been brought to the area during the flooding of the Nile when boats would have been able to take slabs to the site and work in the fields would have been at a standstill until the inundation subsided.

The failure of these gigantic masses of stone to protect the royal cadavers led to a change of approach towards the problem of security. Giza and its pyramids were abandoned as a burial ground and eventually, after many changes, the kings of Egypt were buried in rock-cut tombs in the lonely valley of Biban el-Moluk, an arid desolate spot in the Theban hills. It was here that every Pharaoh of the New Kingdom except for Akhenaten made his eternal home. The tombs were cut into the tawny limestone cliffs, usually starting 69

Below: The god Bes in the forecourt of Dendera. This jolly dwarf-deity was a household protector and helper of women in childbirth.

Right: Osiris shown as a mummified figure wearing a transparent cloak on a plinth in the temple of Isis with the goddess standing behind him.

with steep steps leading down to long descending passages which finally gave way to a series of rooms. Here and there false doors, deep pits and portcullises of great wedges of stone like those used in the pyramids were placed to prevent the access of robbers. As with the pyramids these devices failed to achieve their purpose. The position of the tombs and the value of their contents were known to a wide variety of people – priests, mourners, masons, workmen, funeral furnishers and the like – and all were plundered after the burials. Indeed, even amateur robbers could easily locate the position of the tombs by the huge mounds of debris that came from their excavation. This debris did, however, on one occasion act as an effective shield; the entrance to Tutankhamun's tomb was obliterated by the enormous amount of rubble which came from the tomb of Ramesses VI and flowed over the smaller tomb of Tutankhamun, covering it to a great depth. But even here, when Carter entered the tomb on 24 November 1922, he discovered that the seals had been broken; when he finally saw the burial chamber he found the contents scattered in total confusion by the plunderers, though enough was left behind to astonish the world.

The walls of the rock-cut tombs were covered with texts and illustrations designed to help the deceased in his progress towards immortality in the after-life. As well as this wealth of material there were also the papyrus texts and funerary equipment in the tomb chambers, but as these were now far from civilization and supposedly hidden safely from the world it was necessary to build funerary temples at a distance from the tombs so as not to indicate their whereabouts; here the proper prayers and rites for the deceased could be observed. These mortuary temples were constructed on the edge of the cultivation on the west bank of the Nile where the true desert begins. Each temple had a chamber containing a statue of the dead Pharaoh, which in event of the loss or disintegration of the mummy would provide an alternative resting place for the 'Ka' or vital force of the king. It was most important that the 'Ka' should recognize its owner and it was therefore necessary to give the statue a realistic appearance. These mortuary temples and shrines were for the deceased and not to be confused with the temple buildings and sanctuaries which were dwelling places for the gods. Prayers and food for the deceased were made at the mortuary temple, which sometimes attained great importance. At Medinet Habu, the mortuary temple of

Right: King Alexander offering to Amen-Re in the form of Min, god of fertility, in Luxor temple.

Overleaf: Ptolemy VIII shown adoring Hathor and Harpocrates, Philae.

Ramesses III was not only used for daily services for the Pharaoh but in the Late New Kingdom became the administrative centre of the whole Theban Necropolis. The mortuary temples were inscribed with the deeds of the deceased whilst he was alive and also showed him making prayers and offerings to the gods. In addition they contained stelae or tomb-stones on which were inscribed prayers and scenes calculated to help the deceased towards his goal of eternal life. Frequently these showed the dead man seated before an offering table piled high with food.

The temple buildings for the living, such as those at

Left: Hathor-headed capital in the mortuary temple of Hatshepsut at Deir el-Bahri.

Philae, were the dwelling places of the gods, with whom the Pharaohs could communicate in these sanctuaries. The siting of the temples was most important, and the Pharaohs themselves laid the four corner bricks by means of astral observations. As a rule the temple was set in a sacred enclosure surrounded by mud-brick walls. Two tall pylons with embrasures for flag-poles marked the entrance, and beyond lay an open court. The court in turn led to a pillared hall usually surrounded by small rooms for the storage of temple equipment and for subsidiary rites. The Egyptians knew of the arch but used it only in brick construction and so the distance between the pillars supporting the temple ceiling could not be longer than the heavy stone beams would permit — some ten to fifteen feet. Small openings were left in the roof to admit light, but the interiors must have been very dark and mysterious. In certain cases obelisks stood before the temple, their points covered with electrum, a mixture of gold and silver, reflecting the light of the sun-god on the temple. In Abu Simbel the position of the temple was such that the morning sun streamed through the doorway lighting up the interior. Twice a year, on the mornings of 23 February and 23 October, it penetrated 180 feet into the depths of this rock-cut temple to shed its sacred beams on the four gods in the inner sanctuary, Ptah, Amen-Re, Ramesses the Great and Re-Harakhty, who sit in equal dignity on a massive stone throne. It was the inscription of Ramesses' thousand-ton statue in his funerary temple, the Ramesseum at Thebes, that Diodorus fancifully interpreted as: 'I am Ozymandias, King of Kings. If any would know how great I am, and where I lie, let him excel me in any of my works.' On this Shelley based his poem 'Ozymandias':

> I met a traveller from an antique land
> Who said: 'Two vast and trunkless legs of stone
> Stand in the desert . . . near them, on the sand,
> Half sunk, a shattered visage lies, whose frown,
> And wrinkled lip and sneer of cold command,
> Tell that its sculptor well those passions read
> Which yet survive, stamped on these lifeless things,
> The hand that mocked them, and the heart that fed.
> And on the pedestal these words appear:
> 'My name is Ozymandias, king of kings:
> Look on my works, ye mighty, and despair!'
> Nothing besides remains. Round the decay
> Of that colossal wreck, boundless and bare,
> The lone and level sands stretch far away.

Left:Hathor and Harpocrates receive offerings from Ptolemy VIII, whose figure has been obliterated by the Copts. Temple of Philae.

Right: Ptolemy VIII offers wine to Isis in her temple at Philae.

Below: Ptolemy VI offers milk to Horus at Philae.

The order of the daily temple ritual is preserved for us on the walls of many temples, including Philae. The late Professor Černý gives an excellent account of the liturgy in his book, *Ancient Egyptian Religion*.

> Before entering the temple the priest had to purify himself in the sacred pool. On his arrival at the temple he first kindled a fire and filled a censer with burning charcoal and incense. He then proceeded towards the shrine in which the god had spent the night. He broke the clay seal on the door, pushed away the bolts and opened the two wings of the door. The statue of the god appeared to him and the priest saluted the god, casting himself upon the ground before the statue. He then chanted one or more hymns and offered honey to the god, burning more incense while making four circumambulations around the statue. Alternatively he offered the deity a figure of Maet, the goddess of Truth. Finally he took the statue out of the shrine, removed the old clothing and anointed it with unguent.

After this the toilet of the god or gods takes place.

> [The priest] again censed the deity and sprinkled it with water out of four *nemset*-vessels and four red vessels. After repeating the censing he cleaned the statue's mouth with three different kinds of natron and dressed it with the head-cloth and garments of various colours, replaced its jewels, anointed it and painted its eyelids with green and black eye-paints. Finally he invested the gods with the royal insignia.

Next followed the repast.

> The priest . . . purified the altar and then laid food and drink before the god. He raised each course separately, offering it to the god. The banquet finished, he closed the door of the shrine and sealed it. He purified the room, removing his footsteps with special care and left the room. At every stage in the ceremony the priest recited the appropriate words or formulae.

Ideally this ritual should have been performed by the Pharaoh, but for practical purposes he appointed a priestly deputy except perhaps on great occasions on the principal feast days.

The priesthood in the temples was divided into two orders consisting of 'Prophets' (servants of god) and 'ordinary priests' (pure ones). Theoretically the Pharaoh was high-priest in every temple, but in fact the duties were carried out by the 'First Prophet'. The ordinary priests were divided into four groups, called phyles, and each group served in the temple for one month at a time. The phyle on duty was

Right: Part of the astronomical ceiling in the outer Hypostyle Hall at Dendera, showing some of the boats representing the Hours of the Night interspersed with signs of the Zodiac.

Right: Representation on the ceiling of a corridor in the tomb of Ramesses VI. A ram-headed deity stands in a boat made of a serpent and an elongated double-headed human figure. The god is unnamed and the figures accompanying him in the boat are mythical and enigmatic

responsible for the day-to-day running of the temple and its members received payment partly from the temple revenues and partly from the daily offerings to the gods. The temples were great landowners and the administration of their estates and revenues required large non-priestly staffs. Gifts and endowments to the temples built up over the centuries and vast areas of Egypt were donated by grateful monarchs to swell the enormous wealth of the priesthood. Evidence suggests that during his reign Ramesses III was able to give about one-tenth of the cultivable area of Egypt to the temples.

The daily service was the principal act of worship in the temple and in it the public had no part. Access to the inner parts of the temple was denied to everyone except the priesthood attached to the temple and the Pharaoh or his representative. Apart from a few favoured persons, who may have been allowed into the outer courtyard, public participation was limited to the great festivals. Some of the more important were the Coming-forth of Min, the god of fertility, at harvest time and the festival at Abydos celebrating the revenging of the death of Osiris which provided a dramatic occasion for the re-enactment of this famous legend. Festivals

Below: A pillar in the forecourt of the temple of Kom Ombo adorned with a crowned vulture.

were held when visits were made by one god to another in a neighbouring sanctuary. During the Festival of Opet, held in Thebes in the second month of the inundation, the god Amun sailed from Karnak to Luxor to celebrate his union with the divine mother Mut in the Luxor temple, an occasion for popular excitement. Later in the season Amun left Karnak for the Festival of the Valley where the god visited the mortuary temples on the west bank. The Sed-Festival, held at Memphis, was the most important one in the life of the Pharaoh. This celebrated his thirtieth anniversary on the throne of Egypt. The union of Egypt under one crown was re-enacted and the authority of the Pharaoh renewed. After this the Sed-Festival was repeated at three-yearly intervals and all the gods of the land came to Memphis to pay homage to the Pharaoh. The Nile was frequently in use for such occasions and the procession of sacred boats carrying Horus of Edfu to his marriage with Hathor of Dendera must have been a spectacular occasion. At Philae regular visits were paid every tenth day by Isis to the tomb of her husband Osiris on the island of Bigeh.

Ordinary people, apart from attending the great festivals more for the 'fun of the fair' than for any pious reasons,

Below: Part of a scene showing funeral preparations with embalming priests wearing the jackal masks of the god Anubis. From a New Kingdom tomb.

probably had little contact with the great gods, but they followed secondary cults and magical practices of their own. One of the most popular deities was Bes, a fat little dwarf with a large leonine head who not only brought happiness into the home but protected the occupants against snakes and other terrors and helped the women in childbirth. Other cults were those of Astarte, Anat and Qadesh, brought back to Egypt by soldiers returning from Asiatic wars and by foreign prisoners and craftsmen. Popular cults also arose from the reputations of famous men. Perhaps one of the most striking was the worship of Imhotep for his unique qualities as a physician and a sage. Amulets for the living were also in great demand. Among them, carved on hippopotamus ivory, were representations of Bes, Horus the Child, Isis and Thoeris, a goddess shown as a pregnant female hippopotamus standing on its hind legs. Like Bes this deity was revered as the protectress of women in childbirth.

The most important addition to the gods of Egypt was the god Sarapis, introduced from Macedonia by Ptolemy I to further his hold on the country. The new god was a combination of Osiris and the Greek god Zeus and was represented by a bearded man wearing a *modius* or cylinder-shaped head-

dress. Osiris was already a composite god identified with Apis, the sacred bull of Memphis, having a son Horus and a wife Isis who was also equated with the goddess Hathor. All these gods were now considered to be a triad, so that Sarapis, although a single god, was also considered to be a trinity. The cult of Sarapis was established in a huge temple four miles from Memphis, where his statue with its golden head and jewelled eyes struck awe in the hearts of worshippers as it gazed out of the darkened shrine.

In the religious hot-house of Alexandria, where people came from all over the known world, there was a tendency to assimilate foreign gods with their Egyptian counterparts. Where differences were too distinct the difficulty was overcome by calling them different aspects of the same god. (The Jews and Persians alone resisted this tendency and remained faithful to monotheism.) Alexander the Great, Caesar, Antony and all the Ptolemies were deified, while the Egyptian belief in life after death was to play a major part in the worship of Sarapis, who was spoken of as raising the dead and being a saviour of mankind. In the mysterious darkness of his temple candles were burnt before him and before Isis, who held the infant Horus in her arms. Wax models of parts of the body needing succour were hung about the shrine of Isis. She, as the wife of Osiris and Queen of Heaven, became highly popular and attracted many devotees. Horus was also popular; he was the only son of Osiris-Sarapis and he was also the sun god; the *scarabaeus* with wings outstretched was his symbol. The scarab, or dung beetle, was sacred because of its habit of carrying a mud ball in its front legs – the ball was identified with the sun. Horus finally joined his father and is shown in the Book of the Dead pleading for the deceased.

The worship of Sarapis spread widely throughout Europe in the third and second centuries B.C. and anticipated the ritual that was to appear in the Christian era. Unlike the cult of Sarapis, the essential idea of Christianity, as of the teachings of Buddha, was a new concept of universal unselfish love, but the garments it wore were woven in the cult of Sarapis and Isis and in the rituals of the Egyptian temples. The contribution to Christian thought and practice was considerable. It was natural for Christians to see parallels with the New Testament in the personality of Horus, and thence to identify Mary with Isis. The elevation of Mary to a quasi-divine rank was therefore a natural step. It was also natural for Christianity to adopt almost unconsciously the practical

86

Below: An Egyptian obelisk in Rome bearing on its point a Christian cross.

methods of the popular religion of the time. Christian priests and monks took to head-shaving and wearing the characteristic garments of the Egyptian priests because these seemed to be simple distinguishing marks. One accretion followed another until the original teaching, like that of Buddha, became buried under subsequent acquisitions. Like Buddha, Jesus was made a god. Paul of Tarsus, who had never met Jesus, preached the ancient religion of priest and altar. Jesus became a sacrificial figure offered to God as an atonement for sin to save mankind. The teaching that the renunciation of

self is its own reward became secondary to the priestly ritual. As H. G. Wells says in his *Outline of History:* 'One can imagine the amazement of some earnest Nazarene who had known and followed his dusty travel-worn Master through the dry sunlight of Galilee, restored suddenly to this world and visiting, let us say, a mass at St Peter's at Rome, at learning the consecrated wafer upon the altar was none other than his crucified teacher.' Six centuries later Mohammed founded Islam, the last great religion of the world. With the example of the other great religions before him he was careful not to claim personal divinity; instead he provided a pattern of worship of one God without priests or ambiguous symbolism. No human or animal images were allowed in the mosques; he recognized the temptation of people to venerate such objects and turn them into gods. It was a strong simple religion and eventually came to power in Egypt in 640 after Mohammed had died when the army of Islam conquered the country.

The gods of Ancient Egypt were coming to the end of their long reign, but it was not the decrees of emperors so much as the new religion of Christianity that brought about their downfall. The Holy Family took refuge in Egypt after fleeing from Herod and it is reputed they found shelter in the crypt of the church of Saint Sergius in Cairo during the Roman occupation. The altar in the crypt is still an object of reverence and its white marble is covered with names of visitors, many of them Moslem, who still pay their respects. Tradition holds that at the well at Mataria near Cairo the Holy Virgin washed the Infant's clothes. In A.D. 45 St Mark was reputed to have converted a shoemaker of Alexandria called Annianus to the new religion. Seventeen years after that first conversion the good Saint was martyred in Alexandria by the Romans for protesting against the worship of Sarapis. The Emperor Hadrian is reputed to have written, 'Their one god is nothing peculiar', but he was to be proved wrong. The refusal of the Christians to admit that the Emperor was god resulted in some 140,000 believers perishing for the cause. This appalling persecution defeated itself, and in the year 331 Constantine recognized Christianity as the official state religion. Thereafter the new religion became more intolerant and the destruction of the civilization of Ancient Egypt began. The great statue of Sarapis and his temple were destroyed. The old rites and writings were forbidden and the hieroglyphs soon became meaningless to the early Christians

of Egypt; the monuments they covered were pagan, and en-

Right: A Coptic cross appears on a column in the temple of Isis at Philae. It has been cut deeply into a frieze of hieroglyphs including ankhs, symbols of eternal life in Ancient Egypt.

thusiastic monks went indefatigably about their task of destruction. The results of their labours with hammer and chisel are all too plainly visible on the ancient temples; no carving was too high, no sanctuary too secluded to escape their blind intolerance. At Philae the Copts choked the colonnades and courtyards with their hovels and pulled down many of the temples for building material.

In the reign of Theodosius the Great (A.D. 379–395) Christianity was declared to be the religion of the Empire. The Serapeum in Memphis was destroyed and Christian inscriptions became more general, but the cult of Isis continued when the other gods and goddesses of antiquity had been forgotten. Pilgrims from Greece and the Roman Empire came to worship her, heaping her shrine at Philae with offerings as late as the fifth century A.D. Owing to her, Philae was the last stronghold of paganism. Her hymn states: 'I am the mother of all nature, mistress of all the elements, origin and principle of the centuries, supreme divinity, queen of the spirits, first among the inhabitants of the sky, unique among the gods and goddesses; the luminous summits of the sky, the salutary breezes of the sea, the desolate silences of hell, it is I who govern all at my will.'

Finally in 577 the temple was converted into a Christian church and Byzantine crosses were engraved on the walls amongst the reliefs of Isis, Osiris and Horus. The ancient stones of the quay and other buildings were torn down to build two convents on the east bank of the Nile and a small basilica on the island. The beautiful carvings were patiently chiselled away and the island became cluttered with the dwellings of the Copts. For twelve centuries the story of the world's first great civilization was lost. In 639 Egypt was conquered by the army of Umar and became an isolated part of Islam until the arrival of the Napoleonic expedition in 1798. There were few travellers during this period and the history of Philae remained obscure, but there was lively interest in holy places, and pilgrims at their peril made their way to Philae where Isis shared her temple with the Virgin Mary.

CHAPTER THREE
THE PTOLEMIES

Philae, temple of the Ptolemies, was begun by Ptolemy II, Philadelphus (285–246 B.C.) and completed in essentials by Ptolemy III, Euergetes, but its decoration with inscriptions and carvings continued throughout the whole of the Ptolemaic period and indeed was never quite finished.

The Ptolemies were Macedonian Greeks who had no previous ties with Egypt but who were welcomed as liberators after the Persians, who had dominated the country since 525 B.C., surrendered to Alexander the Great in 332 B.C. Altogether there were fifteen Ptolemies, beginning with Soter ('Saviour'), and seven Cleopatras (the name means 'Glory to her father'). The last Ptolemy was Caesarion, the son of Cleopatra VII and Julius Caesar, and with the deaths of himself and his mother the rule of the Pharaohs over Egypt came to an end and the country became a province of Rome directly under the rule of the Roman emperor. There were thirty Dynasties or families before the Ptolemies. King Menes was the first king of the First Dynasty which ruled Egypt from about 3100 to 2890 B.C. Before this Egypt was made up of small principalities which slowly became organized into two kingdoms: one of the Upper Nile to the south, known as the White Kingdom, and one of the Lower Nile or Delta in the north, known as the Red Kingdom. These two Egyptian kingdoms were for a time hostile to each other but were eventually united under the rule of King Menes. The emblems of the united kingdom were represented by the union of the lily for Upper Egypt and the papyrus for Lower Egypt. The ruler was styled 'King of Upper and Lower Egypt' and 'Lord of the Two Lands'. He wore a double crown consisting of the White Crown of the south and the Red Crown of the north. King Menes was regarded not only as a king but also as a god, and all the kings who followed him were gods to their Egyptian subjects.

Alexander the Great (356–323 B.C.) was the son of Philip II of Macedonia and Olympias, an Epirote princess. His father 91 was a practical genius and his mother a visionary given to wild outbursts of prophecy. The boy was fortunate in having his education directed by Aristotle. In 336 B.C. his father was assassinated and Alexander gained the kingdom against all other claimants. After consolidating his position at home he proceeded against the Persians and defeated Darius III at the battle of Issus and followed this by conquering Syria and Palestine, which cleared the way for his entry into Egypt. Egypt was the last of the Mediterranean provinces to be won. The Egyptians did not defend their country; they regarded Alexander as a liberator from Persian tyranny. During the winter of 332–331 B.C., which he spent in Egypt, Alexander went to the Oasis of Siwa (near the site of his new city) which contained a shrine dedicated to the god Amun. Here the priests pronounced him to be the son of the god, a title that he made no effort to refuse, although for everyday affairs he remained the son of his father Philip. In accepting this title he paved the way for the Ptolemies, who all became god-kings in their turn. During this short period he also founded the city of Alexandria in a splendid position on the Canopic mouth of the Nile. It was to become for a while the centre of the civilized world, with its famous library and the Mouseion, the first university in the world. It also possessed one of the wonders of the ancient world, the Pharos. This lighthouse, designed by Sostratus during the reign of Ptolemy II, Philadelphus, in the third century B.C., was made of white marble and the fire on its 400-foot summit was visible thirty-four miles away.

Alexander continued his conquests as far as India but here his weary troops refused to go any further than the river Beas. Disappointed he commenced the long journey home, but he was never to see home again. At Babylon he caught a fever from which he died in 323 B.C., but not before his Macedonian soldiers had passed one by one through his chamber to bid him farewell.

After the death of their great leader the generals quarrelled amongst themselves for the inheritance of his conquered kingdoms. In Egypt Ptolemy, son of Lagos, a Macedonian nobleman, won the day; as well as being one of Alexander's most trusted generals, he was a brilliant statesman. He limited his rule to Egypt, a wealthy country whose people had been accustomed to autocratic rule for centuries. He followed the example of Alexander in accepting the position of Pharaoh and had himself portrayed in the temples worshipping the Egyptian gods. He further established his

Right: Upper and Lower Egypt, represented by the lily and papyrus, are tied in union by the Nile gods at Abu Simbel.

importance by securing his late leader's body and having it buried with great splendour in a magnificent tomb in the centre of Alexandria. To begin with, Ptolemy carried on the government of Egypt for the Macedonian King Philip Arrhidaeus and after him for Alexander II, son of Alexander the Great, but on the latter's death he assumed full control, and the Ptolemaic Dynasty was founded in 304 B.C., Ptolemy I taking the title Soter I, Saviour.

A great deal of Ptolemy Soter's reign was occupied by wars with his colleagues who were still dividing Alexander's empire. He was successful in establishing an Egyptian protectorate over Cyprus and in securing his western flank by taking Cyrenaica. At home he reorganized the army and administration on Macedonian lines, producing an efficient fighting machine and a smooth-running government. New concepts of art were introduced from the Greek world via Greek traders and soldiers and had a profound effect on age-old traditions, changing the stylized Egyptian forms into more human terms. Soter I was careful not to allow any of the strange gods from Greece to displace the deities of Ancient Egypt and in many cases the foreign gods became manifestations of the Egyptian gods. Some of the greatest temples,

Above: The goddesses of Upper and Lower Egypt, Nekhbet and Buto, crown one of the Ptolemies in the temple of Isis at Philae.

94

including Philae, Dendera, Edfu and Esna, were constructed during the Ptolemaic period and in the reliefs on these temples the Ptolemies are shown as Pharaohs in the Ancient Egyptian manner with their names and royal titles written in hieroglyphs inside cartouches. Their outlook, however, remained Greek and they spent much of their time developing commerce, building new ports and improving the agricultural system. They were also enthusiastic patrons of learning and one of their finest memorials was the Great Library founded by Ptolemy I.

In 285 B.C. Ptolemy I abdicated in favour of one of his younger sons, born of his third wife Berenice. Ptolemy II, later known as Philadelphus, Lover of his Sister, reigned from 285 to 246 B.C. He revived the Egyptian custom, later followed by many of his successors, of marrying his sister, who became his second wife Arsinoe II. Ptolemy I died two years later at the age of 84. He had been a shrewd and cautious king and left his son a compact and well-ordered realm. Philadelphus had a delicate constitution and, although the sphere of Ptolemaic power was extended during his reign, he was more interested in patronizing the arts and keeping a splendid court at Alexandria. Indeed this has been compared, in its dissolute magnificence, to the court of Versailles under Louis XIV. Philadelphus had many brilliant mistresses but as well as enjoying the artificial life of the court he was responsible for commencing the building of the temples at Philae, and he appears with Isis on the gateway leading to her temple. He was also interested in science and learning and doubled the number of volumes in the Great Library from 200,000 to 400,000. These volumes were not bound as today but kept in rolls, so that every time a phrase was checked the whole roll had to be unwound until the required passage was revealed, then re-rolled and returned to its place. Indexing was unknown but copies of the volumes were made in the Museum, where perhaps a hundred could be made at one time by scribes writing from dictation. Intellectual and artistic pursuits flourished alongside a more scientific approach to agriculture. Foreign strains of wheat and vines were imported and a rotation of crops introduced. More efficient methods gave greater yields.

Ptolemy II was followed by his son Ptolemy III, Euergetes, the Benefactor (246–221 B.C.). He was the son of his father's first wife Arsinoe I. The title Benefactor resulted from conquests he made in Babylon and Persia from which he returned not only with vast hoards of treasure but also with 95

Above: Coin showing head of Ptolemy I.

statues of Egyptian gods which had been captured on previous occasions by the Persians. At sea his fleet controlled the seaboard as far as Thrace, and nearly all the eastern Mediterranean came under Ptolemaic control. As well as being a successful warrior Euergetes was equally noted for completing the building of the temple of Philae and for his interest in science and the arts. He endeavoured to trace the source of the Nile, but in this, like everyone else until modern times, he was unsuccessful. He was the last of the great Ptolemies and when he died Egypt was at the zenith of her power and Alexandria the most cultured city in the world.

Ptolemy IV, Philopator, Father Lover (221–205 B.C.), was the son of Euergetes. He began his reign by murdering his mother and possibly also his father. His rule marked the beginning of the decline of the Ptolemies: in-breeding was having its effect. The new Pharaoh surrounded himself with male and female favourites who indulged his vices and conducted the government as they pleased. However, some elements of courage remained and he fought off an attack by the Seleucids, the descendants of Alexander's general Seleucus who had occupied Syria, but at the cost of Upper Egypt becoming mutinous. Like his father he was a patron of the arts, and he built a temple to Homer and the temple of Arsenuphis at Philae where he is depicted worshipping Isis and Horus. He ruthlessly eliminated anyone who might have mounted the remotest challenge to his position, his uncle and his younger brother Magas joining his mother in the grave. This was to set a pattern for his successors, except that the women of the Dynasty were to prove themselves just as murderous and cruel as the males.

Ptolemy V, Epiphanes, God Manifest (205–180 B.C.), was the son of Philopator and Arsinoe III, and was not more than five years old when he succeeded to the throne. By the time he came of age most of Egypt's foreign possessions had been lost. The country was governed by a series of regents, but owing to a revolt in Alexandria his guardians were obliged to resign their office. Advantage of these circumstances was taken by Antiochus the Great of Syria and Philip V of Macedon to invade the foreign possessions of Egypt. Antiochus won Palestine in the battle of Panium and after concluding peace with Egypt gave his own daughter Cleopatra to Epiphanes to wife. She became the first Cleopatra. Later, when war broke out between Antiochus and Rome, Egypt sided with the latter and Ptolemy V built the shrine to Imhotep at Philae, where he is shown adoring the god.

Right: Ptolemy V, Epiphanes, offers his sceptre to Isis in her temple at Philae.

Overleaf: The half-submerged front façade of the first Great Pylon of the temple of Isis at Philae. It is 150 feet wide and sixty feet high and covered with figures of Ptolemy XII, Neos Dionysos with Isis, Hathor, Horus and other gods.

Ptolemy VI, Philometor, Lover of his Mother (180–145 B.C.), was the eldest of Epiphanes' two sons. He succeeded as an infant under the regency of his mother Cleopatra I, and he appears on the screen walls of the Birth-house at Philae. His mother's death was followed by a break between the Ptolemaic and Seleucid courts on the old question as to which of them should have Palestine. Antiochus IV, the fifth king of the Seleucid Empire, invaded Egypt and – before being ordered off African soil by Rome – captured Philometor, who was followed by his son Ptolemy VII, Neos Philopator, New Father Lover, in 145 B.C. The Alexandrians then put Ptolemy VIII, Euergetes II (145–116 B.C.), on the throne. He murdered his nephew and married the boy's mother, Cleopatra II. He later married his niece, Cleopatra III, who in her turn on the death of Ptolemy VIII murdered Cleopatra II. Cleopatra III was eventually killed by her son. The names of Cleopatra II and III appear in the Greek inscription on the base of the Philae obelisks, which are described in the account of their decipherment by Mr T. G. H. James on pages 177–9.

Euergetes II was a savage, ruthless monarch nicknamed Physcon, Fatty, on account of his bloated appearance. This was the worst period of Ptolemaic rule, and incest and murder were systematically used to ensure that power remained inside the family. No crime was too terrible to preserve their position; no possible claimant to the throne was allowed to live; sons murdered wives, mothers, sisters and brothers to ensure their personal continuity of rule. In the midst of this murderous intrigue the Pharaoh found time to complete the temple to Hathor on Philae which was begun by Ptolemy VI. It reflects the sensuous life of the court, with scenes of music and dancing, drinking and feasting. Ptolemy VIII was the last Pharaoh except for Cleopatra VII to enforce internal peace on Egypt, but to achieve this he called on Rome to subdue his rebellious relatives. The habit of appealing to Rome for help placed subsequent rulers in a vulnerable position, which in the end led to total dependence. Finally expelled by a revolt, Ptolemy VIII sought refuge in Cyprus, while his wife Cleopatra II reigned in Egypt under the title Philometor Soteira, Mother Lover, Saviour. The gallery on the eastern side of the forecourt in the temple of Isis at Philae is ascribed to him.

After the death of Ptolemy VIII his throne was shared by his widow Cleopatra III and her son Ptolemy IX, Soter II, Saviour II (116–107 B.C.), who also had the nickname

Right: Ptolemy VI, Philometor, and his sister wife Cleopatra II before the god Khons, who inscribes the king's name on a palm stalk, attended by Haroeris and Sobk, at Kom Ombo.

Overleaf: The same scene as on pages 98 and 99 after the pumps have removed the water, revealing the eastern colonnade which was built by Ptolemy IV and Ergamenes, his Nubian contemporary. (Photo: T. G. H. James)

Lathyros, Chick Pea, and was the grandfather of Cleopatra VII. He appears with his Queen in a small room in the eastern pylon at Philae with Isis, Hathor and Horus. Nine years later Soter II was banished and his brother Ptolemy X, Alexander I (107–88 B.C.), became co-regent in his place. Eighteen years later Ptolemy X was expelled and perished in a naval battle, after which Soter II was recalled and immediately murdered his mother. In the midst of this confusion Thebes rebelled. Upper Egypt was often antagonistic to rule from Alexandria. There were few Greeks and many Egyptian priests in the area and whenever there was trouble in Lower Egypt advantage was taken of the situation to revolt. During the reigns of Ptolemies IV and V, the people of Upper Egypt had asserted their independence under a native dynasty. Now Soter II so reduced the city of Thebes after three years of conflict that all that remained was a small town in the midst of great monuments, which survive to the present day to remind the world of her ancient greatness.

After the death of Soter II, Ptolemy XI came to the throne in 80 B.C. with the support of the Roman dictator Sulla, who compelled him to marry his own elderly stepmother, Berenice, who had been in charge of Egypt since her

husband's death. Nineteen days later the new ruler had her murdered, and then the people of Alexandria, who resented Rome's domination, dragged the king from his palace and murdered him in his turn. It was now that the father of Cleopatra VII came to the throne – Ptolemy XII, Auletes, the Flute Player (80–51 B.C.). He was the illegitimate son of Ptolemy IX by a concubine, and he endeavoured to compensate for his bastardy by giving himself the title Philopator, Father Lover. His huge figure is carved on the Great Pylons of the temple of Isis at Philae, showing him delivering a fatal blow to his cowering enemies. Smaller engravings depict him offering incense to Isis and Harpocrates. He also completed the temple of Edfu and began to build the magnificent temple of Dendera.

The world that Cleopatra VII grew up in was controlled by the Romans, and she, like her father, realized that her only chance of survival was to collaborate with them. She was born in 70 B.C. when Caesar was thirty years of age and Antony thirteen. Ptolemy XII also gave himself the titles Theos Philopator Philadelphus Neos Dionysus, The God, Lover of His Father, Lover of His Sister, the New Dionysus. He had six children, the eldest being Cleopatra VI, Tryphaena, then Berenice IV, Cleopatra VII, a fourth daughter Arsinoe

Below: Ptolemy VIII, Euergetes II, crowned by the goddesses of Upper and Lower Egypt, Nekhbet and Buto, in the temple of Kom Ombo.

*Right: Ptolemy VIII,
Euergetes II, and
Cleopatra offer sceptres
to Haroeris at Kom
Ombo.*

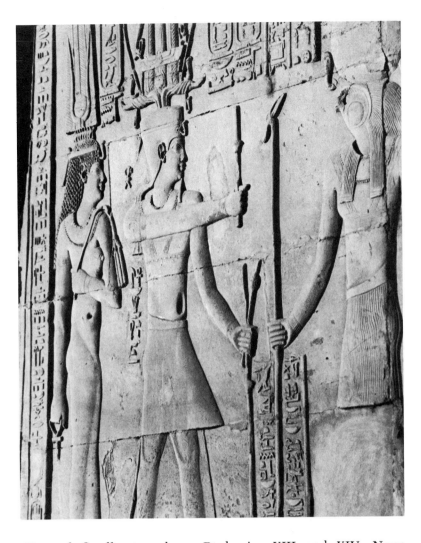

*Overleaf: The front of
the second Great Pylon
in the temple of Isis. It
is 105 feet broad and
forty feet high. On
either side of the central
doorway, as in the first
Great Pylon, are deep
grooves for flag-staffs.
On the walls Neos
Dionysos offers incense
to Hathor and other
gods in the presence of
Isis, Osiris and Horus.*

IV, and finally two boys Ptolemies XIII and XIV. None
were to die natural deaths. The wife of the Flute Player
was also his sister, Cleopatra V, Tryphaena, who may
have been the mother of Cleopatra VII. To retain the support
of the Romans Auletes had to bribe them with huge sums
of money, and the new taxes he imposed plunged the
country into revolt. He had to flee to Rome, leaving the
throne to his eldest daughter, who was soon deposed in turn
by Berenice IV. Now Auletes was returned to power with
Roman aid and promptly had his daughter executed. Cleopatra VII was fourteen at this time; as heir-apparent to her
father's throne, she must have pondered deeply these grue-
some lessons in power politics.

The Greek gods were gradually becoming equated with or
assimilated by the gods of Egypt – Dionysus with Osiris,
Aphrodite with Isis and these in turn were associated with 105

the king and queen. The Egyptians had always believed that the king was the earthly manifestation of Horus in life and Osiris in death. The queen was the god's wife Isis, with whom Cleopatra VII passionately identified herself. Osiris and Isis were not only husband and wife but also brother and sister, and this supported the brother-sister marriages which were so common amongst the Ptolemies and also in earlier Egyptian dynasties. Scarcely a temple exists in Egypt that does not bear reference to the Ptolemies, in some cases not always to their credit. In Philae there is an inscription engraved by two of Auletes' male partners in lechery.

In about 52 B.C. Auletes drew up his will leaving his throne to Cleopatra, now aged eighteen, and his eldest son Ptolemy XIII, aged about ten. Both of the children took on the title Philopator, Father Lover, in addition to the one given to them by their father, Philadelphus, Lover of Their Brothers or Sisters. Pompey was appointed guardian to the new monarchs by the Roman Senate. As Ptolemy XIII was a minor, local guardians were also appointed to look after him. They were an unpleasant trio: Achillas, commander of the army; Theodotus, who was to see to the boy's education; and Pothinus, a eunuch and minister of finance. They plotted

Below: The court of the temple of Kom Ombo. In the background the Great Hypostyle Hall decorated by Ptolemy XII, Neos Dionysos.

to get rid of Cleopatra and use the young king for their own ends. At the same time another trio was breaking up in Rome. The triumvirate of Caesar, Pompey and Crassus was too ambitious to remain together. Crassus was killed at the battle of Carrhae and his army destroyed. Pompey was defeated at Pharsalia in Thessaly, and the Egyptians, who up to then had relied on his support, now found themselves faced with the prospect of backing Caesar. Ptolemy XIII under the guidance of his three guardians had banished his sister Cleopatra VII, who fled to Syria where she rallied supporters to help her regain her throne.

The subsequent story of Cleopatra is well known, but it may be useful to recapitulate the main points since her identification with Isis was central to the cult whose main temple was at Philae.

Pompey and his wife Cornelia now sought help from their Egyptian friends. They arrived in their galley at Pelusium where the Egyptian army confronted Cleopatra. Whilst Pompey waited in his ship for the Egyptians to meet him, the three guardians decided they would lure him ashore and kill him. This was to prevent him supporting Cleopatra and also to protect them from Julius Caesar, who, they supposed, would be under an obligation to them for destroying his enemy. Pompey was rowed ashore in a small boat with Achillas and a Roman officer called Septimus, who had once held command under him. As soon as the boat touched land Pompey was stabbed in the back and the murderers hacked off his head. His unfortunate wife watched the terrible scene from the galley, which immediately put to sea to avoid being taken by Egyptian warships. Four days after this cold-blooded murder Caesar arrived in Alexandria. It was 27 July, 48 B.C. He was greeted by Theodotus bearing Pompey's head and a request that he should leave Egypt, but Caesar was not impressed by this treacherous murder and dismissed the bearer abruptly. He had no intention of leaving Egypt, which was a rich country whose money he needed. The vast sums which the Flute Player had offered for protection were still owing to Rome. Also, under the will of Auletes, it was Caesar's duty to ensure that Cleopatra and her brother should be joint rulers.

Although Caesar had only four thousand men in his command he immediately summoned Ptolemy XIII and Cleopatra to Alexandria, where he was staying in the palace. Cleopatra arrived first, evading her brother's army and guards and finally, history records, reaching the great man's

Overleaf left: Detail of the falcon-headed Horus of Edfu, as it appears on the first Great Pylon at Isis.

Overleaf right: During partial submersion the only way of entering the vestibule to the sanctuary in the temple of Isis was by boat and even this was impossible at high water.

109

chamber wrapped in a roll of bedding carried by a Sicilian merchant called Apollodorus. Cleopatra was aged twenty-one and Caesar an experienced fifty-two, but so captivated was he by her that he took her side against her brother, even though Ptolemy XIII had the backing of the army and the Alexandrian political leadership. In the ensuing hostilities the Egyptians suffered severely and Ptolemy XIII was drowned whilst trying to escape across the Nile. Caesar now arranged that Ptolemy XIV, Cleopatra's other half-brother and now husband, should become joint ruler with her.

Having brought these affairs to a satisfactory conclusion Caesar, probably at the request of Cleopatra, decided to make a voyage up the Nile to show the Egyptians the might of Rome and her support for their appointed rulers. Some four hundred ships formed a spectacular armada and thousands of troops went with them. The royal barge in which Caesar and Cleopatra travelled was three hundred feet long, sixty feet high, and fitted out in the most sumptuous manner. The temples glowing with colour and the movement of the priests and people, the great flagstaffs gay with banners and the electrum-tipped obelisks glittering in the brilliant sunshine, must have made a deep impression on the royal couple, who

Below: The sacred lake at Dendera, known as 'Cleopatra's Bath'.

were also the gods Isis and Horus on the way to their temple of Philae. Soon after they returned to Alexandria Caesar left for Asia Minor; he had been less than nine months in Egypt but he left behind an unborn son who was to be called Caesarion, Little Caesar, and to become Ptolemy XV, the last of the Dynasty.

A year later, in 46 B.C., Cleopatra took Caesarion and her husband Ptolemy XIV with her to stay as Caesar's guests in Rome. She wanted to assure the continued support of Rome for her throne, and this she achieved. Alas, time was running out for Caesar; on 15 March, 44 B.C., he was stabbed by his fellow senators and fell mortally wounded at the foot of the statue of his old enemy Pompey. Two days later his will was read, but it contained nothing regarding Cleopatra or Caesarion. Mark Antony's supremacy after Caesar's death was challenged by Octavian, Caesar's great-nephew, who was named as his heir in his will and immediately assumed the name Gaius Julius Caesar. Cleopatra's child had been given the title Caesar before Octavian, and this now placed his life in peril. Cleopatra, her hopes of sharing the throne with Caesar shattered, lost no time in returning to Egypt with Caesarion and her husband. Ptolemy XIV did not long

Below: Marcus Aurelius offers an elaborate pectoral to Sennuphis (divine wife of Haroeris) in the outer corridor at Kom Ombo.

survive; he was killed to make way for Caesarion. For the new reign Cleopatra not surprisingly dropped the title Philadelphus, Brother Loving, but retained Thea Philopator, The Goddess Who Loves Her Father. Ptolemy XV was called Theos Philopator Philometor, God Who Loves His Father and Mother. Cleopatra had these titles inscribed on the temple of Dendera where she and Caesarion were represented as Pharaohs.

In the struggle for power that followed Caesar's death, Antony and Octavian set about dividing the Roman Empire between them. Antony was now recognized in Egypt as the New Dionysus and he sent for Cleopatra to come to him at Tarsus. Cleopatra welcomed the invitation. Fate had given her another chance to become queen of the Roman world and she set sail for Tarsus determined to win Antony to her side. Plutarch's vivid description in his 'Life of Antony' makes clear the symbolic significance of the event:

> She relied above all upon her physical presence and the spell and enchantment which it could create . . . She came sailing up the river Cydnus in a barge with a poop of gold, its purple sails billowing in the wind, while her rowers caressed the water with oars of silver which dipped in time to the music of the flute, accompanied by pipes and lutes. Cleopatra herself reclined beneath a canopy of cloth of gold, dressed in the character of Aphrodite (Venus), as we see her in paintings, while on either side to complete the picture stood boys costumed as cupids who cooled her with their fans. Instead of a crew the barge was lined with the most beautiful of her waiting-women attired as Nereids and Graces, some at the rudders, others at the tackle of the sails, and all the while an indescribably rich perfume, exhaled from innumerable censers, was wafted from the vessel to the river-banks. Great multitudes accompanied this royal progress, some of them following the queen on both sides of the river from its very mouth, while others hurried down from the city of Tarsus to gaze at the sight. Gradually the crowds drifted away from the market-place, where Antony awaited the queen enthroned on his tribunal, until at last he was left sitting quite alone. And the word spread on every side that Aphrodite had come to revel with Dionysus for the happiness of Asia.

Like Caesar before him Antony was captivated by Cleopatra, but there was more to their alliance than fleshly union. It was an alliance of gods. Antony was the New Dionysus, the immortalizing god, and Cleopatra was Aphrodite. Dionysus was equally the Egyptian Osiris and Aphrodite

Right: Domitian offers milk to Hathor, who suckles her son Horus. The scene is inscribed on the Propylon at Dendera.

was Isis, the sister-wife of Osiris. Cleopatra was thus the incarnation of Isis upon earth and Isis was the greatest of all the deities of the Graeco-Roman world, revered as widely and as passionately as Dionysus and loved with greater intensity. Her worship spread beyond the bounds of Egypt, and relics have been found as far afield as England, France, Spain, Italy, Germany, Greece and Turkey as well as in her native Egypt. In the Sistine Chapel in Rome we can look at Pinturiccio's frescoes in the Room of the Saints and there gaze at a group which includes Moses, Hermes Trismegistus and Isis, and also at Io, the Greek cow seen turning into the Egyptian Isis. As R. E. Witt says in his book, *Isis in the Graeco-Roman World:* 'For countless numbers of men and women in the Graeco-Roman world Isis remained what she had been in the black land of the Pharaohs: Mistress of the World in the Beginning, Mistress of Eternity, Source of Grace and Truth, Resurrection and Life, the Supreme Deity as Maker of Monarchs and Mother of God.'

Cleopatra's first demand from Antony was for the death of her half-sister Arsinoe IV, the last of the Flute Player's children apart from herself. From Tarsus the lovers sailed to 115

Left: Caesarion and Cleopatra VII on the rear wall of the temple of Dendera.

Egypt where they lived in great luxury during the winter of 41–40 B.C. This ecstatic interlude was brought to a close by news from Rome that Antony's wife Fulvia and brother Lucius Antonius had launched a rising against Octavian in which they had been utterly defeated. Antony on arrival in the capital managed to reach an agreement with Octavian which was sealed by his own marriage to Octavia, Octavian's sister, made possible by the opportune death of Antony's wife Fulvia. While this was happening in Rome Cleopatra was giving birth to Antony's twins, Alexander Helios and Cleopatra Selene, in Egypt. Antony's marriage to Octavia must have been a disastrous shock for Cleopatra; once more it must have seemed that the fate of Egypt and the Ptolemaic Dynasty were in the hands of an outsider and that in spite of all her efforts Egypt would become a province of the Roman Empire.

Antony now decided to commence his Parthian campaign and asked Cleopatra to join him in his conquest of the east, which was to be followed by war against Octavian for the Roman Empire. It was already three and a half years since Cleopatra had seen Antony, but whatever she may have felt about his desertion of herself and his children, she once more set out to meet him. Antony needed Cleopatra's advice and, above all, the wealth of Egypt and her army and navy. He took the title Autocrator, Ruler Absolute, and promised to restore Egypt to its former glory and to recognize Caesarion as legal heir to the Empire. Alas for Cleopatra's hopes, the campaign was a disaster in which almost half Antony's army perished. Relations with Octavian worsened and, in 31 B.C., the stage was set at Actium for the last battle. The Egyptian fleet was defeated but Antony and Cleopatra escaped with about one-third of their ships and sailed for Egypt. Once she was in Alexandria Cleopatra's first concern was to ensure the continuity of her line. With this in mind she celebrated the coming of age of her son Caesarion, now aged sixteen and bearing the title conferred upon him by Antony, King of Kings, Ptolemy XV. It is strange to think of Antony putting Caesar's son in front of his own by Cleopatra, but it was politically practical and a small return for all the help Cleopatra had given him. Cleopatra now arranged that Caesarion should proceed to the safety of India with his tutor Rhodon and part of the royal treasure. She also began to plan her own emigration to the east where she hoped to found a new oriental kingdom.

Octavian's forces were closing in on Egypt. On 1 August, 117

30 B.C., Antony's fleet set out to engage the enemy ships, whilst his army took up positions to defend Alexandria. However, both fleet and army surrendered without a fight and Octavian entered the city as conqueror. Cleopatra, on hearing the news, shut herself up in her mausoleum with her treasure, accompanied by her hairdresser Iras and her lady-in-waiting Charmion. A report came to Antony that she had committed suicide and he then ordered his servant Eros to kill him too, but Eros turned the blade on himself. Antony seized another sword and plunged it into his own body. As he lay dying Cleopatra's messenger came to tell him that she was still alive and wanted him to come to her. Antony was carried to her mausoleum, but the doors were barricaded and he had to be hoisted in great pain and with much difficulty through an upper window. Soon afterwards he died, but not before he had told Cleopatra to put her trust in one of Octavian's staff, Gaius Proculeius. Cleopatra quickly sent for Proculeius, but he, obeying Octavian's instructions, foiled Cleopatra's attempt to kill herself. Deprived of escaping her enemies in death the wretched queen was transferred to the palace under guard, leaving her treasure in Octavian's hands. News now came that Caesarion, fleeing southward, had been betrayed by his tutor and murdered. Cleopatra's hopes were ended; all her long struggle to continue the dynasty and to keep Egypt a separate state had come to nought, and there was nothing left for her except the possible degradation of appearing in chains at a Roman triumph. She decided once more to end her life. Popular legend has it that a snake was smuggled past her guards in a basket of figs, an echo of her original entry into the palace smuggled in a roll of bedding eighteen short years before. Snakes have always been part of the Egyptian heritage and since the uraeus, the Greek cobra head-dress, adorned the Pharaonic crown, she may have had this symbol in mind for her royal death. When Octavian's men reached her chamber they found her lying on a golden couch dressed in her royal robes. She was already dead and Iras lay dying at her feet. Charmion in her final gesture was trying to adjust the diadem on the brow of her mistress. One of the guards cried out, 'Is this right?', and Charmion gave the final epitaph of the dynasty: 'It is entirely right and fitting for a queen descended from so many kings.'

Thus ended the 3000-year reign of the Pharaohs, and with Cleopatra's death Egypt came under direct rule from Rome.

CHAPTER FOUR
PHILAE

Philae itself is an island in the river Nile situated at the beginning or southern end of the First Cataract. At this point, before the Aswan dam was built, the river gathered speed, dropping sixteen feet in swirling eddies and turbulent falls of white water for three miles until the Cataract ended and the Nile resumed its placid flow through the seven hundred miles of desert to the Mediterranean. The island, which has withstood the erosion of the debris-filled river since earliest times, owes its safety to the strength of the crystalline rock of which it is formed. This emergence of the earth's crust occurs frequently here and has provided the enduring stone for the monuments of the country. There are numerous islands in the region – Bigeh, Agilkia, groups of small islands at Awad and El Hasa, and, below the Cataract, Siheil and Elephantine. In early times the priests of Philae claimed that the source of the Nile was bottomless and lay beneath the rocks of Bigeh whence half the river rose to flow north and half to flow south. The priests of Elephantine claimed that the source lay with them, and these rival traditions were kept up for as long as it was possible to maintain them. Certainly the river is over a hundred feet deep in places and anyone who has sailed in a *felucca* through the islands, round Elephantine and Siheil, knows how confusing the direction of the flow appears in the swirling eddies which twist and turn in all directions. Everywhere rocks in grotesque shapes rise from the water, sometimes resembling elephants which may have given the name Elephantine to the island. The wash of the silt-bearing water had polished the granite to a shining dark grey similar in colour to elephant hide.

There is a myth told about Philae. The island is usually called by the local inhabitants Kasr Anas el-Wogud after the hero of one of the tales in the Arabian 'Thousand and One Nights', which had its scene transferred to Philae in the Egyptian version:

The king's son, Anas el-Wogud, fell in love with the vizier's daughter Zahr el-Ward, 'Flower of the Rose'. The two young people met secretly until they were discovered by the imprudence of the maiden's servant. The vizier was enraged and in order to bring the affair to an end imprisoned his daughter in the temple of Isis under close guard. Anas el-Wogud wandered far and wide in search of his beloved and in the course of his wanderings showed kindness and compassion to animals. One day a hermit told him that Zahr el-Ward was on the island of Philae and Anas hurriedly made his way there. Alas, the water surrounding the island teemed with crocodiles, but as he stood lamenting his fate one of the monsters offered to carry him to the island on its back out of gratitude for the prince's previous kindness to animals. On his arrival, birds belonging to his sweetheart told him that she was on the island, but he could never obtain sight of her. Meanwhile 'Flower of the Rose', unable to endure her fate, let herself down from her window by a rope made from her clothes and was conveyed from the island by a compassionate shipmaster. Finally after another long period of search the lovers found one another and with the consent of their families were happily wed.

At the northern end of the Cataract stood the great outpost of Ancient Egypt, the bustling city now known as Aswan. It was the starting-point of the caravan and shipping routes leading to Nubia and the strange unknown country of central Africa, 'The Land of Ghosts'. Through it passed the earliest commercial and military expeditions of the Egyptians. Strategically it commanded the First Cataract, the waterway linking Egypt with Nubia. It was also important for its huge quarries which yielded fine, coloured granite containing a large proportion of translucent quartz and yellow, brown, pink and black mica. Building works were conducted on an enormous scale and King Mycerinus of the Fourth Dynasty actually attempted to obtain enough granite from Aswan to face the whole of his pyramid at Giza, which then stood 218 feet high and had a base length of 356 feet. The east bank of the river swarmed with quarrymen, whose statues and obelisks were sent all over Egypt.

The erection of these enormously heavy shafts is a tribute to the skill and inventiveness of the ancient engineers. At the site a solid foundation was made on top of which a heavy rectangular piece of granite was placed as the base for the obelisk. Along one side of this at a suitable distance from its edge a groove was cut in which the foot of the obelisk could engage. A ramp of earth about half the height of the

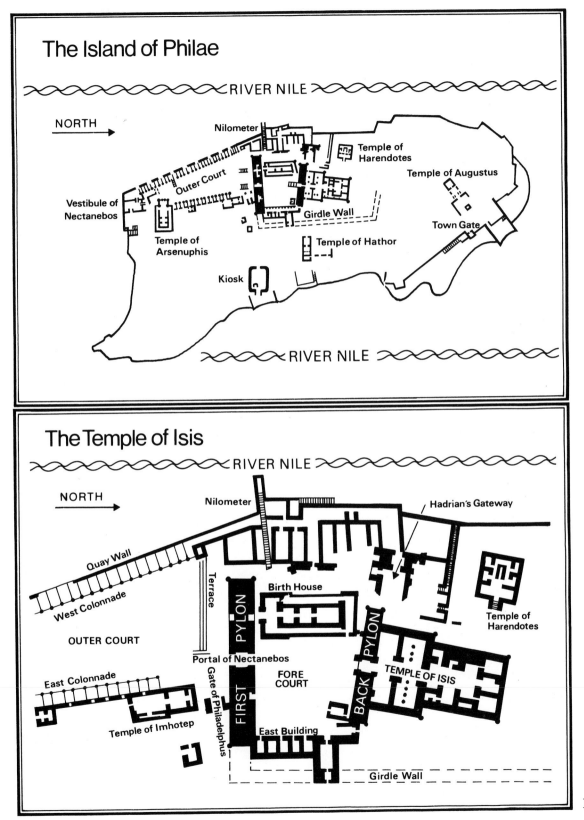

The Island of Philae

RIVER NILE

NORTH →

Nilometer

Temple of Harendotes

Temple of Augustus

Outer Court

Vestibule of Nectanebos

Girdle Wall

Temple of Arsenuphis

Town Gate

Temple of Hathor

Kiosk

RIVER NILE

The Temple of Isis

RIVER NILE

NORTH →

Nilometer

Hadrian's Gateway

Quay Wall

Terrace

Birth House

West Colonnade

FIRST PYLON

BACK PYLON

TEMPLE OF ISIS

Temple of Harendotes

OUTER COURT

Portal of Nectanebos

East Colonnade

FORE COURT

Gate of Philadelphus

Temple of Imhotep

East Building

Girdle Wall

obelisk was now built in such a way that a funnel was left over the base block. Fine sand was poured into the hole until it was partly filled and then the obelisk was dragged up the ramp and its base tipped into the funnel to come to rest on the surface of the sand. Gradually the sand was removed through a tunnel at the bottom of the pit, rather like an hour-glass, and the falling sand allowed the obelisk to slide slowly down until its leading edge fitted into the groove in the base block. It was now possible to pull the obelisk into an upright position.

Upper Egypt was traditionally divided into 22 administrative regions called nomes, the first of these being Elephantine. Here the governor and his officials maintained law and order. It was the military post from which relief expeditions could be sent to beleaguered fortresses on the upper stretches of the Nile. The name Aswan comes from the Ancient Egyptian designation of the place, Sunu (in Greek,

Below: Philae's western side seen from the island of Bigeh. From right to left: the landing stage and pavilion of Nectanebos, the colonnades leading to the first Great Pylon, with the kiosk of Trajan in the background, the Birth House and the second Great Pylon with the sanctuary, and lastly the ruins of the temple of Harendotes.

Syene), which means market. This market was a flourishing trading centre fed by a continuous stream of merchants, caravans and adventurers. Nubians and perhaps Sudanese brought to it all kinds of strange and delightful objects – gold, leopard-skins, ostrich feathers, incense, sandalwood, ebony, ivory, fans, shields made of hide, gazelles, lions, baboons, giraffes, antelopes and cattle. The temple for the gods of the area was also on Elephantine; they were a triad composed of Khnum, the ram-headed god of Elephantine; Anukis, goddess of the Cataract and wife of Khnum; and their daughter Satis, who was the goddess of Siheil and wore a white crown with antelope horns.

Philae, being situated at the head of the First Cataract, provided a pleasant spot for travellers to rest after working their boats and cargoes through the difficult passage of the rapids. That fearless Victorian Egyptologist Amelia Edwards again vividly recalls the difficulties and splendours of the passage:

At Assûan, one bids good-bye to Egypt and enters Nubia through the gates of the Cataract – which is, in truth, no cataract, but a succession of rapids extending over two-thirds of the distance between Elephantine and Philae. The Nile – diverted from its original course by some unrecorded catastrophe, the nature of which has given rise to much scientific conjecture – here spreads itself over a rocky basin bounded by sand-slopes on the one side, and by granite cliffs on the other. Studded with numberless islets, divided into numberless channels, foaming over sunken rocks, eddying among water-worn boulders, now shallow, now deep, now loitering, now hurrying, here sleeping in the ribbed hollow of a tiny sand-drift, there circling above the vortex of a hidden whirlpool, the river, whether looked upon from the deck of the dahabeeyah [native boat] or the heights along the shore, is seen everywhere to be fighting its way through a labyrinth, the paths of which have never yet been mapped or sounded.

Those paths are everywhere difficult, and everywhere dangerous; and to that labyrinth the Shellalee, or Cataract-Arab, alone possesses the key. At the time of the inundation, when all but the highest rocks are under water, and navigation is as easy here as elsewhere, the Shellalee's occupation is gone. But as the floods subside and travellers begin to re-appear, his work commences. To haul dahabeeyahs up those treacherous rapids by sheer stress of rope and muscle; to steer skilfully down again through channels bristling with rocks and boiling with foam, becomes now, for some five

123

months of the year, his principal industry. It is hard work; but he gets well paid for it, and his profits are always on the increase . . .

The scenery of the First Cataract is like nothing else in the world – except the scenery of the Second. It is altogether new, and strange, and beautiful. It is incomprehensible that travellers should have written of it in general with so little admiration. They seem to have been impressed by the wildness of the waters, by the quaint forms of the rocks, by the desolation and grandeur of the landscape as a whole; but scarcely at all by its beauty – which is paramount.

The Nile here widens to a lake. Of the islands which it would hardly be an exaggeration to describe as some hundreds in number, no two are alike. Some are piled up like the rocks at the Land's End in Cornwall, block upon block, column upon column, tower upon tower, as if reared by the hand of man. Some are green with grass; some golden with slopes of drifted sand; some planted with rows of blossoming lupins, purple and white. Others again are mere cairns of loose blocks, with here and there a perilously balanced top-boulder. On one, a singular upright monolith, like a menhir, stands conspicuous, as if placed there to commemorate a date, or to point the way to Philae. Another mass rises out of the water squared and buttressed, in the likeness of a fort. A third, humped and shining like the wet body of some amphibious beast, lifts what seems to be a horned head above

Below: The same scene as on the previous page –at mid-water. The high-water marks are plainly visible.

the surface of the rapids. All these blocks and boulders and fantastic rocks are granite; some red, some purple, some black. Their forms are rounded by the friction of ages. Those nearest the brink reflect the sky like mirrors of burnished steel. Royal ovals and hieroglyphed inscriptions, fresh as of yesterday's cutting, start out here and there from those glittering surfaces with startling distinctness. A few of the larger islands are crowned with clumps of palms; and one, the loveliest of any, is completely embowered in gum-trees and acacias, dôm and date palms and feathery tamarisks, all festooned together under a hanging canopy of yellow-blossomed creepers.

In ancient times travellers made their devotions at Philae before continuing through the dangerous territory of the south to the 'Land of Ghosts'. Everywhere the rocks and temples bear witness to their prayers. Nearby on the island of Siheil are more than two hundred and fifty rock inscriptions dating from the Fourth Dynasty down to Ptolemaic times. Pepi I, as early as c. 2280 B.C., cut canals through the cataract to assist the boat crews on their way to the calm water above Philae. It was to the 'Land of Ghosts' that Herkhuf, a seasoned explorer, went on his fourth expedition during the ninety-year reign of Pepi II, c
The account of his adventure is recorded on the façade of his

tomb on the west bank of the Nile opposite the island of Elephantine. On this occasion he returned with a pigmy from Central Africa. When Pepi heard the news he wrote him a letter which said:

Come northward to the court at once. Thou shalt bring this dwarf with thee that thou hast brought alive, prosperous and healthy from the Land of Ghosts, for the dance of the god, to gladden and rejoice the heart of the King of Upper and Lower Egypt, Neferkare, Pepi II who liveth for ever. When he goes down with thee into the vessel, take care lest he should fall into the water. When he sleeps at night appoint excellent people to sleep beside him in the tent, inspect him ten times a night. My Majesty desires to see this dwarf more than the gifts of Sinai and of Punt. If thou arrivest at the court, bringing this dwarf with thee alive and prosperous and healthy, my Majesty will do for thee a greater thing.

An inscription on the island of Siheil is of the Ptolemaic period but describes a seven-year famine that occurred during the reign of Djoser, the king who built the Step Pyramid, c. 2670 B.C. The king complains that 'the Nile has

not risen for seven years and that there is a scarcity of corn. There are no vegetables and no food of any kind, every man is stealing from his neighbour. Counsellors have no advice to give and when the granaries are opened nothing but air issues from them.' The king in great distress asks the chief lector-priest of Imhotep: 'In what place does the Nile rise? What god dwells there, that I may enlist his help?' The priest replies that he will consult the sacred writings in the temple of Thoth at Hermopolis. In due course he returns to the Pharaoh and tells him that there is a city in the middle of the Nile called Elephantine, which is the seat from which Re despatches life to everyone. It is the source of life, the place from which the Nile leaps forth in its flood to impregnate the lands of Egypt. On the east side of the city are great mountains containing hard stone which is used in the temples of Upper and Lower Egypt. The priest continues that the god of the place is Khnum, who allots the lands of Egypt to each god and controls the grain, the birds, the fish and everything on which they live. Some days later, King Djoser had a dream in which the great god Khnum appears. The king does everything he can to render the god favourable, but Khnum replies: 'I am Khnum your maker; with my arms I protect you and help you. You should be building temples and restoring my statues and those buildings that have fallen into ruin; I am Nun who has existed from earliest times; I am the Nile flood who runs at will; my sanctuary has two gates from which I let out the water for the flood.' Khnum continues that he will make the flood rise for the king, that want will cease and the granaries be filled. When the king awoke he remembered the dream and set about restoring the damage that had been done. He decreed that large tracts of land on both sides of the river stretching from Elephantine south should be given to the temple of Khnum. In addition one-tenth of all produce and livestock raised was to be given to the temple, and also taxes on caravans and gold mining. 'Such are the terms of my decree,' said King Djoser, 'and I order that it be inscribed on a stone set up in a sacred place, and I also order that the priests shall make my name live eternally in the temple of Khnum, Lord of Elephantine.' An identical decree is to be found in the temple of Philae, so it seems that the priests of Philae continued to maintain parity with their rivals.

The small island of Philae lies four miles south of Elephantine, just beyond the Aswan Dam. It measures 500 yards from north to south and 160 yards from east to west and is 127

Left: The colonnades leading to the first Pylon and flanking the Outer Court.

almost entirely covered with temples and monuments which were protected from the river by high walls, quays and terraces. Part of the foundations of these ancient constructions rest on the underlying granite and the remainder are deeply set into the earth. The oldest monument on the island is the altar built by Taharqa and referred to on page 145. The earliest standing building was erected by the last Pharaoh Nectanebos II (360–343 B.C.). This temple stands on the southern end of the island immediately over the water, and of its original fourteen pillars only six remain. Here Hathor welcomes the visitor from her place on top of the lotus capitals. Her serene head with its cow ears supports the architrave, but the roof has long since disappeared. The space between the columns is filled with stone screens over six feet high, crowned with concave cornices and rows of

Below: The first Great Pylon shows the half-submerged figures of Ptolemy XII, Neos Dionysos smiting his enemies in the presence of Isis, Horus and Hathor.

Overleaf: The exterior of the west wall of the sanctuary of Isis.

uraeus-serpents. The screens are carved with reliefs showing Nectanebos sacrificing to the gods. The vestibule leads into the Outer Court which is bounded on the west by the Quay Wall and its hundred-yard-long colonnade. This contains a row of thirty-one (formerly thirty-two) columns, its capitals taking the form of flowers, remarkable in their variety with no two being alike. The windows in the wall overlook the water and the island of Bigeh. Most of the columns show carvings of Tiberius offering gifts to the gods. The ceiling, which is partly destroyed, is decorated with stars and flying vultures. The rear wall has two rows of bas-reliefs of Tiberius and Augustus offering to the gods. A subterranean stairway leads from the first part of the colonnade to a small Nilometer.

The temple of Arsenuphis or Iry-hemes-nufer is to the right of the Vestibule of Nectanebos and begins the East Colonnade. It was built by Ptolemy IV, Philopator, and extended by Epiphanes. The reliefs show Ptolemy V, Epiphanes, before Isis and other gods, and also Ptolemy IV, Philopator, before Isis, Horus and Unnefer. The shrine is enclosed by a wall which has fallen down in places, and the carvings show Tiberius worshipping Osiris, Isis, Harsiesis, Nephthys, Khnum, Satis, Anukis, Arsenuphis and Tfenet. The East Colonnade is partly roofed and has seventeen columns, only six of which have their capitals completed. Several doorways open through the colonnade wall; the first five lead to the court in which the ruined chapel of Mandulis stands. The sixth opens into the small temple of Imhotep where Ptolemy V, Epiphanes, is seen before Imhotep. Between the temple of Imhotep and the first Great Pylon of the temple of Isis is the Gate of Ptolemy II, Philadelphus, showing the Pharaoh being led forward by Isis.

In front of the Great Pylon lie two fallen Roman lions carved out of pink granite, and here also stood two granite obelisks erected by Ptolemy VIII, Euergetes II, and his second wife Cleopatra III. These are described in detail in the special section at the back of the book. On the base of the eastern obelisk was an inscription complaining to the royal couple that the priests of Isis at Philae were being forced to refund the expenses of civil and military authorities incurred during their stay on the island. This, they said, did not leave them enough resources to continue sacrifices and libations for the welfare of the royal family. The response was immediate; Euergetes II released the priests of Philae from further payments.

129

Overleaf: A general view of the temple of Isis after the lowering of the water. The colonnade of the Birth House can be seen between the two Great Pylons. (Photo: T. G. H. James)

Left: The western side of the first Great Pylon showing the sadly defaced figures of Horus and Isis receiving honours from the Ptolemies.

Below: The rear of the first Great Pylon with the Birth House on the right.

Neither of these obelisks are now in Philae but repose in the garden of Mr Ralph Bankes at Kingston Lacy in Dorset. The story of their long journey throws light on the methods used to provide an insatiable world with the monuments of Ancient Egypt.

William John Bankes, scholar, Member of Parliament, and ancestor of the present Ralph Bankes, first saw the obelisks in 1815. The eastern obelisk lay on its side half-buried and its western fellow was badly damaged and only about a third of it remained. Bankes endeavoured to recover them from the mud and debris, but was unable to do so for lack of proper equipment. He reluctantly left them where they lay but with the firm intention of one day bringing them back to Kingston Lacy.

In the nineteenth century no respectable traveller would venture to return from Egypt without a souvenir of his visit. The ruler at this time was the capable Mohammed Ali (1803–1849), who dispensed *firmans,* or licences, to consuls and important foreigners allowing them to remove valuable pieces of Ancient Egypt in return for favours to modern Egypt. It is probable that Mohammed Ali wondered why foreigners should bother either about these useless old stones, which his people used for making lime, or about the dried cadavers in their crumbling coffins, which the European infidels ground into powder for making medicines. Two of the most avid collectors were the British Consul, Henry Salt, and the

Consul-General of France, Bernardino Drovetti. Mohammed Ali was so generous in the *firmans* he gave to these two men that they eventually had to curb their mutual antagonism and agree to divide the archaeological treasures of Ancient Egypt between them. They gave money and presents to the local chiefs who saw to it that other collectors were warned off or not supplied with labour. Salt was fortunate to have as his agent the 6 ft. 8 in. giant Italian, Giovanni Belzoni, and it was Belzoni that Salt asked to bring the Philae obelisk to Cairo, a monument that he had already agreed to give to Bankes. On hearing of the matter Drovetti claimed that the obelisk belonged to him, but grandly ceded the ownership to Bankes. Belzoni considered that Drovetti had found it impossible to find ways of transporting the obelisk through the cataract and had relinquished his claim for this reason. Belzoni may have been right in his judgment, for the obelisk was twenty-two feet long and weighed six tons.

In 1819 work began and the obelisk was levered and pushed on rollers to a stout wooden pier for shipment. 'But, alas!,' Belzoni writes, 'when the obelisk came gradually from the sloping bank and all its weight rested on it, the pier, with the obelisk and some of the men, took a slow move-

Below: The forecourt of the temple of Isis seen through the doorway; the pillars of the west colonnade are visible. On the right stand the Hathor-headed capitals of the Birth House columns.

Below: Detail of the floral capitals surmounted by Hathor heads which support the roof of the Birth House.

ment, and majestically descended into the river.' Eventually Belzoni and his men hauled it out of the mud and loaded it on to the boat for its journey to Cairo. But all was not yet over. Drovetti's men intercepted Belzoni on his way to Aswan and it was only after a long altercation which ended in gun-fire and the arrival of Drovetti himself that the monument was allowed to proceed on its way to Alexandria. It was shipped to England on the *Despatch* in May 1821. In 1822 Bankes returned to Egypt to collect the remains of the companion obelisk which still lay in the forecourt of the temple. This broken piece was extracted and eventually arrived in England in 1829. The base for the first obelisk was placed in position in Bankes's garden on 17 August 1827, the site being chosen by the Duke of Wellington, who was an old friend of the family. The obelisk itself had to wait a further twelve years before it was placed on the base. This was because it had been damaged in transit and Bankes wished to find suitable stone for the repairs. The needed granite eventually came from Leptis Magna in Libya by the grace of King George IV of England, who had obtained more than he required for the erection of a small temple to grace the royal gardens and gave this stone to Bankes, whom he knew through the Duke of Wellington. The following inscription now appears on the base of the monument:

WILLIAM JOHN BANKES, ESQ. M.P. ELDEST SON OF HENRY BANKES ESQ. M.P. CAUSED THIS OBELISK AND THE PEDESTAL FROM WHICH IT HAD FALLEN TO BE REMOVED UNDER THE DIRECTION OF G. BELZONI IN 1819 FROM THE ISLAND OF PHILOE [sic] BEYOND THE FIRST CATARACT AND BROUGHT THIS PLATFORM FROM THE RUINS OF HIERASYCAMINION IN NUBIA.
THIS SPOT WAS CHOSEN AND THE FIRST STONE OF THE FOUNDATION LAID BY ARTHUR DUKE OF WELLINGTON AUGUST 17 1827.
THE GRANITE USED IN THE REPARATION OF THIS MONUMENT WAS BROUGHT FROM THE REMAINS OF LEPTIS MAGNA IN AFRICA AND WAS GIVEN FOR THIS PURPOSE BY HIS MAJESTY GEORGE IV.
THE INSCRIPTION ON THE OBELISK AND PEDESTAL RECORD THEIR DEDICATION TO KING PTOLEMY EUERGETES II AND TWO CLEOPATRAS HIS QUEENS WHO AUTHORIZED THE PRIESTS OF ISIS IN THE ISLAND OF PHILOE TO ERECT THEM ABOUT 150 YEARS B.C. AS A PERPETUAL MEMORIAL OF EXEMPTION FROM TAXATION.

Above left: The kiosk of Trajan, regarded by many as the chief attraction of the island of Philae.

Below left: Detail of the floral capital of one of the columns of the kiosk of Trajan.

Below: General view of the island of Philae after the water had been pumped out of the coffer dam. (Photo: T. G. H. James)

Left: The kiosk of Trajan with the first Great Pylon of the temple of Isis, showing the eastern door to the forecourt.

Nearby lie the remains of the western obelisk so far un-honoured.

The French Consul Drovetti died in a mental asylum at Turin in 1852. It is ironical that a large part of the antiquities collected by Salt was bought by the French government, while the collection made by the French Consul was acquired by Italy and Germany.

The north side of the Outer Court at Philae is bounded by the first Great Pylon of the temple of Isis. This is 150 feet broad and 60 feet high, consisting of two towers with a gate between them. Deep grooves for flag-poles are cut on either side of the portal. It was begun by Ptolemy II, Philadelphus, and completed in essentials by Ptolemy III, Euergetes I, though the decorations were carried out over a much longer period and indeed were never finished. The temple is the principal sanctuary on the island and is dedicated to Isis and her son Horus, the Harpocrates of the Greeks. On the front of the right or eastern tower stands the huge figure of Ptolemy XII, Neos Dionysos, grasping a band of enemies by the hair and raising his club for the fatal stroke. To the left stands Isis watching the sacrifice with the falcon-headed Horus of Edfu and Hathor. Above are two reliefs: to the right Neos Dionysos presents the crown of Upper and Lower Egypt to Horus and Nephthys; on the left he offers incense to Isis and Horus the child. On the western tower of the Pylon the Pharaoh is seen in the same stance slaying his enemies once more whilst Isis, Horus and Hathor look on. Above this he appears in the presence of Unnefer (the name given to Osiris after his resurrection) and Isis and again before Isis and Hariesis. Unfortunately the reliefs have been severely damaged by the industrious Egyptian Christians, the Copts. Along the whole length of the base of the first Pylon are reliefs of small Nile figures bringing offerings. The main gateway through the Pylon was built by Nectanebos at the same time as he built his small temple and vestibule. On either side of the gateway Coptic crosses have been carved into the sandstone, and in the thickness of the doorway there appear reliefs of Nectanebos in the presence of various gods and the goddess Isis. On the right is a French inscription recording the victory of General Desaix over the Mamelukes in 1799. General Desaix greatly appreciated the treasures of Ancient Egypt, and it was he who spotted the famous Dendera Zodiac when in pursuit of the remnants of the army of Murad Bey. William Bankes also coveted this sixty-ton carving, unique in Ancient Egypt, but the French were 141

Overleaf: A watercolour of Philae painted by Francis Arundale about 1832. The island had stood clear of the Nile until the first Aswan Dam was built by the British in 1902. (Dept. of MSS, British Library)

successful in outwitting other competitors (including Salt and Drovetti) and in cutting the three-foot-thick stone from the ceiling of its shrine in Dendera and transporting it safely to Paris, where it now rests in the Louvre.

Beyond the gateway lies the forecourt of the temple of Isis. On the left or western side is the Birth-house containing scenes of the birth and childhood of Horus. The Birth-house is an essential feature of the temples of the Ptolemaic period. The idea for it may have originated in the representations in the temples of Deir el-Bahri and Luxor of the divine birth of Hatshepsut and of Amenophis III. Starting as an element in the relationship between the reigning monarch and the imperial deity Amen-Re and continuing as an important justification of the divinity of the king, it grew in importance with the remarkable spread of the Osiris cult as the universal religion of Egypt and reached its full development in the Ptolemaic period. These temples were designed to celebrate the rites relating to the Osirian tradition of the child Horus, who grew to manhood after the murder of Osiris and overthrew the enemies of his father. Horus as Pharaoh of Egypt became the ancestor of all succeeding Pharaohs and the prime giver of all law and order in the land. It was therefore essential that each Pharaoh on his accession should be recognized as a true descendant of Horus and a legitimate inheritor of the Horus tradition. In the Sanctuary the Hawk of Horus, wearing the Double Crown of Upper and Lower Egypt, stands in a thicket of papyrus. Below, Isis carries the newly born Horus in her arms. Surrounding her protectively are the gods Thoth, Wazet, Nekhbet and Amen-Re. A colonnade surrounds three sides of the Birth-house and the columns have floral capitals surmounted by sistrum capitals with Hathor heads. (A sistrum was a musical instrument rather like a rattle.) The screen walls between the columns show reliefs of Ptolemies VI, VIII, and X, as well as Tiberius, in the presence of various gods.

On the right or eastern side of the forecourt is a graceful gallery of columns with floral and palm leaf capitals which support a cornice, bearing a row of uraeus-serpents. The inscription assigns the building of the gallery to Ptolemy VIII, Euergetes II, but the carvings on the walls show Ptolemy XII, Neos Dionysos, before the gods. Six doorways lead through the rear wall of the colonnade to small rooms which were used for practical purposes connected with temple worship: storing religious equipment, preparing incense, keeping the sacred books and perhaps the priestly regalia.

Right: The defaced lintel of the doorway through the first Great Pylon, showing several figures of Nectanebos before various deities.

144

On the south side, the forecourt is bounded by the rear of the main gateway and the rear walls of the first Great Pylon. On the right or western tower Ptolemy XII, Neos Dionysos, stands before Osiris, Isis and other deities, and below this two sacred boats are carried in procession by priests. On the left or eastern tower, Ptolemy XII, Neos Dionysos, stands before Amun, Mut and other gods. A small doorway in this Pylon leads to a room with reliefs showing Ptolemy IX, Soter II, before Isis, Hathor and Horus, and his Queen and the Princess Cleopatra before Isis. Over another small doorway are reliefs of Ptolemy XII, Neos Dionysos, accompanied by the standards of the nation. This opens to a stairway leading to the roof from which there is an excellent general view of the island. In the south-east corner of the forecourt stands the earliest work at Philae, the granite altar of Taharqa, the Ethiopian Pharaoh of Napata around 670 B.C.

The northern wall of the forecourt is formed by the second Great Pylon which is 105 feet broad and 40 feet high and is set at a different angle to the first Pylon. An inclined plane of shallow steps leads to the gateway between the towers. At the base of the right or eastern tower part of the granite foundation of the island protrudes and this has been carved into a stele on which Ptolemy VI, Philometor, and his

Left: The rear view of the second Great Pylon taken from the vestibule.

Queen Cleopatra II stand before Isis and Horus. An inscription refers to the grant of the *Dodekaschoinoi* made to Isis, which brought the priests of Philae into parity with the priests of Elephantine, who had received a similar grant. '*Dodekaschoinoi*' is the Greek for 'twelve *schoinoi*', a *schoinos* equalling about seven miles. The *schoinos* was not a measurement of area but of length, so presumably meant seven miles of the river Nile, including the arable land.

On the left or western tower Ptolemy XII, Neos Dionysos, offers incense and dedicates sacrificial animals to Horus, Hathor and other gods. Above are two small reliefs, terribly mutilated, of Neos Dionysos presenting a wreath to Horus and Nephthys and offering incense and pouring water on an altar in the presence of Osiris, Isis and Horus. On the eastern tower there are similar scenes but in a much better state of preservation.

Both towers, like the first Pylon, have grooves for flag-staffs. The doorway between the towers shows Ptolemy VIII, Euergetes II, greatly defaced before an equally defaced series of gods.

On the east side of the doorway is an inscription to the Christian Bishop Theodorus. The doorway enters a small open court, which is the temple of Isis proper, and leads to her sanctuary. Amelia Edwards described it as follows:

Below: The vestibule leading to the sanctuary of Isis in her temple.

Here is a place in which time seems to have stood as still as in that immortal palace where everything went to sleep for a hundred years. The bas-reliefs on the walls, the intricate paintings on the ceilings, the colours upon the capitals are incredibly fresh and perfect. These exquisite capitals have long been the wonder and delight of travellers in Egypt. They are all studied from natural forms – from the lotus in bud and blossom, the papyrus, and the palm. Conventionalised with consummate skill, they are at the same time so justly proportioned to the height and girth of the columns as to give an air of wonderful lightness to the whole structure. But above all, it is with the colour – colour conceived in the tender and pathetic minor of Watteau and Lancret and Greuze – that one is most fascinated. Of those delicate half-tones, the careful facsimile in the 'Grammar of Ornament' conveys not the remotest idea. Every tint is softened, intermixed, degraded. The pinks are coralline; the greens are tempered with verditer; the blues are of a greenish turquoise, like the western half of an autumnal evening sky.

Below: The submerged eastern entrance to the court between the Pylons.

Right: The sacred boat of Isis at Philae. One of the Ptolemies kneels on the deck, offering to the shrine of the goddess.

The court at one time had a colonnade on its east and west sides and the open space between could be shaded from the sun by a velarium or awning which was drawn or withdrawn across the opening by cords. This little court was separated from the vestibule beyond it by screen walls uniting four columns, behind which four other columns lent their support to the roof of the hall. The reliefs have been replaced on the east side by Coptic crosses before which a Christian altar was erected in about A.D. 600. On the side of the doorway leading to a room on the right is another inscription to Bishop Theodorus, made during the reign of Justinian (A.D. 527–565) and claiming credit for 'this good work'. A similar inscription commemorates the archaeological expedition of 1841 sent by Pope Gregory XVI. One would wish that the good prelates had had a little more humility. Three small antechambers, flanked by dark rooms, lead to the sanctuary which is lit by two small windows. It still contains the pedestal placed here by Ptolemy III, Euergetes I, and his wife Berenice for the image of Isis in her sacred bark.

Surrounding the sanctuary are the Osiris chambers reached by a short staircase on the west side of the temple which leads to the roof and then descends to the first room where the Nile-god offers libations of milk to the soul or 'Ba' of Osiris, 149 sitting before him in the form of a bird. In the second room is the falcon-headed mummy of Osiris. In the third room the god Shu and the Emperor Antoninus, who built the room, stand before Osiris and his two sisters Isis and Nephthys. Another room on the roof shows Isis and Nephthys by the naked body of Osiris, lying on a bier. The frog-headed Heket and the falcon-headed Harsiesis stand by the bier beneath which are four canopic jars for the entrails of the god. The other walls show the corpse of Osiris amongst marsh plants with a priest pouring consecrated water, and the jackal-headed Anubis stands by the bier of Osiris beside which kneel Isis and Nephthys, sisters of Osiris.

Once these scenes were bright with brilliant colours, the columns and capitals scintillating in the clear sunshine against vivid blue skies. Green palm trees clustered on the island and swayed above masses of flowering plants. Every winter thousands of visitors made the trip up the Nile passing wonder after ancient wonder until finally the voyage culminated in the splendour of Philae set above the wild grandeur of the First Cataract. As Robert Curzon wrote: 'Excepting the Pyramids, nothing struck me so much as when on a bright moonlight night I first entered the court of the

Right: The goddess Nekhbet over the papyrus sign for Lower Egypt, at Philae.

Below: The base of the first Pylon is covered with small Nile figures bringing gifts to the temple.

great temple of Philae.' The outside walls of the temple are covered with reliefs largely dating from the reign of Tiberius. On the west side of the temple near the second Great Pylon stand a gateway and a ruined vestibule built by the Emperor Hadrian. On the lintel the Emperor stands before Osiris, Isis and Harsiesis. Within the gateway Marcus Aurelius stands before Osiris and below offers grapes and flowers to Isis. The uncompleted vestibule shows Nephthys presenting the crown of Lower Egypt and Isis the Crown of Upper Egypt to Horus. On one wall is a relief of Osiris being carried on the back of a crocodile across the Nile; perhaps the myth of Anas el-Wogud gained support from this picture. Another relief on the north wall shows Isis, Nephthys, Horus, Amun and Hathor worshipping the Hawk-god rising over the river beneath the island of Bigeh. The island has a vulture

Left: The ruined entrance to the temple of Bigeh.

perched on it and beneath is a cave surrounded by a serpent holding the figure of Hapi the Nile-god representing the source of the Nile. To the north of Hadrian's gateway is a ruined temple built by the Emperor Claudius dedicated to Harendotes, 'Horus-the-protector-of-his-Father', one of the many forms of Horus.

The most northerly part of the island contains the ruined temple of Augustus which was built in the eighteenth year of his reign. Here was found a stone bearing the trilingual inscription of Cornelius Gallus, now in the Cairo Museum. He was the first Roman Prefect appointed after the death of Cleopatra VII and was successful in suppressing the revolt of the Egyptians in 29 B.C. The stone celebrates his victory. Beyond this temple is the town gate of Philae, with steps leading down to the Nile.

This progression round Philae has taken a clockwise direction starting in the south and proceeding up the west side to the northern end, returning down the east side to the temple of Hathor built by Ptolemy VI, Philometor, and Ptolemy VIII, Euergetes II. It stands just east of the second Great Pylon of the great temple and consists of a colonnaded hall and forecourt. The colonnade was decorated by Augustus and is filled with carvings of festivities in recognition of Isis and Hathor, the Aphrodite of Greece and goddess of all the joys of the senses. The scenes show music and drinking. Augustus offers a festal crown to Isis and flowers to Nephthys. Bes beats a tambourine and plays a harp; an ape plays a lute. Flute-players, harpers, dancing apes flow round the pillars and priests carry in an antelope for the feast.

Further south is the last important monument on Philae, the so-called Kiosk, sometimes called 'Pharaoh's Bed'. The rectangular building is supported by fourteen columns with beautifully carved floral capitals. Only two of the screen walls between the columns are completed. They show the Emperor Trajan burning incense before Isis and Osiris and offering wine to Isis and Horus. This unfinished and uncompleted building is one of the most popular monuments of Philae.

Immediately to the west of Philae lies the island of Bigeh, where according to legend the left leg of Osiris was buried after his body had been cut up by his brother Seth. The Greeks called the tomb Abaton, beneath which it was believed the Nile took its source, part of the water, as legend records, flowing north and the remainder southwards into Nubia. Once every ten days and on annual festivals Isis left 153 her temple of Philae and visited the tomb of her husband. The burial place was surrounded by 365 altars on which the priests laid daily offerings of milk. Two inscriptions on the walls of Hadrian's Gateway at Philae describe the ritual and say that fishing, fowling and music were prohibited in the area. No one except the priests on duty were allowed into the sacred grove, and people in the vicinity were warned to speak in whispers whilst the religious ceremonies were in progress.

Philae and her treasures, too long submerged, will shortly rise from the Nile once more to reveal 'their perfect grace and exquisite proportions'. Perhaps it is right to quote Amelia Edwards's farewell after she had visited the island in its original glory:

> It has been a hot day, and there is dead calm on the river. My last sketch finished, I wander slowly round from spot to spot, saying farewell to Pharaoh's Bed – to the Painted Columns – to every terrace, and palm, and shrine, and familiar point of view. I peep once again into the mystic chamber of Osiris. I see the sun set for the last time from the roof of the Temple of Isis. Then, when all that wondrous flush of rose and gold has died away, comes the warm afterglow. No words can paint the melancholy beauty of Philae at this hour. The surrounding mountains stand out jagged and purple against a pale amber sky. The Nile is glassy. Not a breath, not a bubble, troubles the inverted landscape. Every palm is twofold; every stone is doubled. The big boulders in mid-stream are reflected so perfectly that it is impossible to tell where the rock ends and the water begins. The Temples, meanwhile, have turned to a subdued golden bronze; and the pylons are peopled with shapes that glow with fantastic life, and look ready to step down from their places.
>
> The solitude is perfect, and there is a magical stillness in the air. I hear a mother crooning to her baby on the neighbouring island – a sparrow twittering in its little nest in the capital of a column below my feet – a vulture screaming plaintively among the rocks in the far distance.
>
> I look; I listen; I promise myself that I will remember it all in years to come – all these solemn hills, these silent colonnades, these deep, quiet spaces of shadow, these sleeping palms. Lingering till it is all but dark, I at last bid them farewell, fearing lest I may behold them no more.

CHAPTER FIVE
THE FATE OF PHILAE

The fate of Philae has concerned Egyptologists since the old Aswan Dam was built by the British during the years 1898 to 1902. The dam was a large undertaking even by modern standards, for it is over a mile long, 130 feet high and 100 feet thick at the base. When its 180 sluice-gates were closed the trapped Nile waters flooded 140 miles back to the Sudanese border. The height of the dam was at first restricted because of the protests made by people interested in preserving Philae and other temples and monuments from submersion. Winston Churchill remarked ironically of the preservationists at the time: 'This offering of 1,500 millions of cubic feet of water to Hathor by the Wise Men of the West is the most cruel, the most wicked and the most senseless sacrifice ever offered on the altar of a false religion. The State must struggle and the people starve, in order that the professors may exult and the tourists find some place to scratch their names.'

Before the building of the dam the island of Philae had always stood clear of the river, safe on its granite foundation against the turbulent rush of the flood with its abrasive silt. Once the dam went into operation the annual inundation trapped by it covered Philae for nine months of each year, and the temples remained partially submerged until the sluice-gates were opened in March to release the silt-laden water to the parched farmland of Egypt. After the end of November, when practically all the valuable suspended silt had passed through the sluices and the water was comparatively clear, the gates were gradually closed and the lake above the dam was allowed to fill until it reached its peak in February and the cycle of irrigation recommenced.

In 1895, before the Aswan Dam was built, the engineer in charge, Captain Henry Lyon, was asked to underpin the monuments of Philae so that they could withstand the submersion. This he did; he also excavated part of the site where he discovered the remains of some Christian churches. 155

As it turned out the submersions were not altogether bad; they saved the temples from erosion by sand-storms and helped to remove salt deposits which were injurious to the stonework. Regular inspections of the site showed that it had suffered less damage than might have been expected. The paintwork had of course been washed away but the stones had remained in position, and as the water only receded during the hot summer months when tourists were at a minimum the temples were to some extent protected from the attentions of souvenir hunters. The present removal of the monuments gives another opportunity for excavating the site as well as the unexplored ground beneath the temples, a bonus for the salvage operation.

Below: Flashback to Abu Simbel – in the process of being re-erected. Beyond the colossal figures of Ramesses the Great rises the steel reinforcement for the huge arch which will bear the weight of the artificial cliff behind the statues.

In 1955 fate once again struck Philae. To support the rapidly increasing population of Egypt President Gamal Abdel Nasser decided to construct the Saad-el-Aali, the High Dam. On 14 May 1964 he and the Soviet Prime Minister Nikita Khrushchev together pressed the button which blew up the sand barriers protecting the diversion channel, and for the first time in history the course of the great river was altered by man. The High Dam was completed in 1971, and since then the water contained by it has reached a height of 597 feet above sea level, 200 feet higher than the old Aswan Dam. The construction of the new dam was comparatively straightforward. On the east bank of the river a deep diversion channel was cut through the solid rock. This led to six

Right: The joins between the replaced stones are carefully filled with plaster made from the original sandstone.

intake tunnels through which 14,000 cubic yards of water pass every second to the biggest hydro-electric power station in the world and thence to irrigate the old and reclaimed land of Egypt. The dynamos produce 10,000 million kilowatt hours, double the previous supply.

Once the Nile was diverted its old bed was closed with a rock-fill dam. Rocks cut from the diversion channel were heaped in two rows across the bed about a thousand yards apart and the space in between was filled with desert sand, pumped in a slurry of water from huge deposits in the area. Buried in this sand were large concrete inspection tunnels and down the centre a vast curtain of concrete descended into the granite bedrock to prevent seepage of water through the sand and rock-fill. Once the water had drained away from the sand it was compacted by heavy mechanical rollers which gave it a consistency approaching sandstone. Additional strength was provided by injecting cement under great pressure into the natural crevices and flaws in the surrounding rock; this was especially necessary in the diversion channel area. The width of the High Dam is 1,070 yards at its base and 45 yards at its crest. It is 4,000 yards long and 120 yards high. This huge construction contains the

Below: The façade of the King's temple at Abu Simbel before work commenced. Sheet piles for the coffer dam lie in the foreground. The entire temple was carved in one piece from the living rock. In the centre is a statue of Re-Harakhty, the falcon-headed god of the horizon, to whom the temple is dedicated.

equivalent in material of seventeen pyramids the size of the Great Pyramid of Cheops. Enough metal has been used in the gates, sluices and power plant to build 15 Eiffel Towers. As the Egyptian workmen rightly sang, 'We built the pyramids, we will build the Saad-el-Aali.'

The great advantage of the High Dam is that it can store surplus water over a period of years, thus balancing low floods with high, something that would have appealed greatly to King Djoser. It will give two million extra acres of arable land to Egypt and five million to the Sudan. This irrigation will not be seasonal as in the case of the Aswan Dam but will be continuous throughout the year and every year, thus providing additional cropping. Against these gains is the loss of the valuable silt which will now sink to the bottom of the lake and at most increase the freshwater vegetation for the benefit of the excellent Nile fish. It is estimated that in some five centuries' time the silt will fill up the lake, but perhaps by then some other means of water conservation may have become available or the climate of the country may have changed back to its lush pre-desert state. Already the evaporation from the two thousand square miles of lake surface, reckoned at 7 per cent and

representing 6,200 million cubic yards annually, has caused unusual clouds and haze in the surrounding area. The raising of the water table will increase the size of distant oases and possibly produce new ones. The absence of silt in suspension in the lake will cause the water to lose its famous eau-de-nil colour and become blue, which will be very acceptable to tourists for winter sailing, water-skiing, fishing and swimming. Although the silt is lost it will be replaced by chemical fertilizers already being produced with the abundant supply of cheap electricity.

Whilst the High Dam was one answer to Egypt's problem of feeding her ever-growing population it presented a very grave threat to the existence of Philae, the only temple complex between the two dams. The temples were now caught in the artificial lake between the dams and kept permanently in an almost submerged position. Much worse, they were subjected to a daily rise and fall of several yards. This tidal movement would inevitably end in the erosion and destruction of the temples. If Philae were to be preserved international action was necessary fast. Between 1959 and 1968

Below: Part of the sheet-piled coffer dam surrounding the island of Philae.

consideration was given to a number of plans for saving the temples. Two schemes merited special attention. The first, proposed by the Egyptian engineer Osman Rostem, was supported by the government of the Netherlands. This plan was to isolate the island from the rest of the reservoir by a series of small dams linking the islands of Bigeh and Agilkia with the bank of the Nile to form a protective barrier behind which Philae could rest in a lake of her own, where the height of the water could be maintained at the most suitable level. This scheme, like the similar French one for Abu Simbel, was finally rejected in favour of the present project, which is to transfer the monuments stone by stone to the nearby island of Agilkia. There they will be re-erected in positions similar to those they previously occupied, but on a site safe above the new water level.

Philae and Abu Simbel were the most important temples to be threatened by the High Dam, but many monuments, villages and cemeteries have been affected by the rising waters, which now stretch southwards for over 300 miles and form a lake with an average width of eight miles and a

Above left: The uncompleted power-house of the High Dam in 1967.

Below left: Today the Nile gushes from the largest hydro-electric station in the world.

Below: The coffer dam round the temples of Abu Simbel keeps out the rising water with only a few feet to spare.

Left: The sheet piling round the island of Philae is complete except for this last gap through which can be seen the kiosk.

depth of 100 feet. Some of the ancient ruins have been saved by UNESCO and great efforts have been made by archaeologists from all over the world to excavate and assess the sites before they were covered. Much useful information was obtained in the short time at their disposal. The work was greatly encouraged by the government of Egypt, which allowed a part of the excavated material to be kept by the participating countries. Some of these rewards were more scientific than artistic. At Gebel Adda, opposite the temples of Abu Simbel, a large Meroitic Christian and Moslem cemetery was excavated by the Smithsonian Institution in Washington, and a great many objects including crates of skulls and skeletons were taken to America for further examination. This cemetery dates from about 500 B.C. and now lies lost to the world beneath 200 feet of water.

The work at Philae was subject to all the problems and difficulties which beset great operations of this kind and is being carried out by the UNESCO Executive Committee of the International Campaign to save the Monuments of Nubia. Perhaps the most daunting task confronting the Committee was the raising of the necessary finance to pay for the project. This was again greatly helped by the government of Egypt's offer of antiquities to the forty-four States which participated in the preservation of the ancient monuments. Italy, the Netherlands, Spain and the U.S.A. each received a temple, Debod being allocated to Spain where it is to be re-erected in Madrid. Smaller antiquities going to other States will be shown in their respective museums.

Many appeals had to be made before the world recognized the value of saving these historic treasures, but eventually widely differing countries provided money to enable the work of salvage to go ahead. At UNESCO headquarters in Paris a group of international experts assembled to consider measures for preserving not only Philae but other treasures of the world's cultural and natural heritage. The result of their meetings is that the rescue of Philae is being carried out by Egyptian engineers assisted by Swedish, French, German and British consultants. The cost will come to some £7½ million, of which a magnificent £650,000 was raised by the Exhibition of the Treasures of Tutankhamun at the British Museum. The boy king has been a great asset to the preservation of his ancient kingdom as well as a splendid ambassador for Egypt. The Treasures of Tutankhamun have already been to the United States and Japan and will also be seen in Russia before returning to the United States to be shown in

Overleaf: The temples of Abu Simbel safely re-erected above the now blue Nile. The sediment which gave the colour 'eau-de-nil' to the world has sunk in the still waters of Lake Nasser.

165

New York. The Egyptian authorities responsible for the saving of Philae are H. E. Dr Gamal Moukhtar, Vice-Minister of Culture, Mr Ahmed Kadri, Director-General of the Organization for the Preservation of Nubian Monuments, and Dr W. S. Hanna, the chief engineer. As René Maheu, the Director-General of UNESCO, has said: 'By positive awareness of a universal cultural heritage, mankind recognizes its own oneness in time and space, and proclaims the unity of its destiny through the centuries and the nations.'

The contractors for the saving of Philae are the High Dam Authority and Condotte d'Acqua and Mazzi of Italy. The High Dam Authority is responsible for the construction of the coffer dam and pumping out the water inside the dam. It will also prepare the re-erection site on the island of Agilkia and will have it suitably landscaped. These operations will cost approximately £2½ million. The two Italian companies are responsible for dismantling the monuments, transporting them to the new site and re-erecting them. Agilkia is a granitic island 500 yards north-west of Philae. Here 340,000 cubic yards of rock have been blasted from the top and tipped down its eastern side to extend the available surface and to give the island the approximate shape of Philae. Bulldozers will level the surface so that the monuments and temples may be re-erected in similar positions relative to those they occupied on Philae.

In March 1972 work was started on building the coffer dam round the island; this was the most difficult part of the operation. A double row of 320,000 sheet piles, each fifty feet long, had to be driven through mud and silt until they reached the rock bottom of the river. The corridor between them then had to be filled with 800,000 cubic yards of sand, which fortunately is situated in vast accumulations only three miles away. Some of the sand was carried by barges but most was loosened by jets of high pressure water and the resulting slurry pumped through pipes to the site. Here it was directed into the twenty-foot space between the double row of sheet piles. The water escaped through the narrow joints of the piles leaving most of the sand in position. This gift of sand from the sea has been of enormous value to modern as well as to Ancient Egypt. But the gifts of the sea and of the Nile would have been of little value if the Egyptians and Nubians had not toiled to make use of them. The strange nature of the country and its dominant river had long accustomed them to short bouts of excessively hard work. In the little Nubian villages, now submerged, the only

168

time available for crop planting was between inundations when for a short three months strips of land would appear in the bed of the river as the water receded. During this time the industrious Nubians had to sow and harvest their scanty crops. The escarpments on which their villages stood were too high to be flooded by the river and, apart from a few carefully irrigated and built-up fields, all was desert. The building of the High Dam and the rescue of Abu Simbel, Philae and the other temples would have been impossible without their hard-working co-operation.

Once the sand was properly compacted in the coffer dam, the pumps which served to pump the sand and water slurry were used to drain the temples. The water was reduced by about ten inches a day until the island was clear of the Nile for the first time since the High Dam was built. When the temples emerged they dried out in the hot sun and the accumulations of mud and algae were carefully brushed off

so that the carvings and inscriptions could be recorded by photogrammetry. This is a photographic process that produces an accurate picture in depth of the subject and enables exact reproductions to be made if such necessity occurs. Once this is safely completed the temples will be dismantled. As in Abu Simbel every piece of stone will be marked and numbered so that it can be replaced in exactly the same position in relation to its fellows when it comes to be re-assembled. The upper stones will naturally have to be removed first and carefully placed in order to await the removal of all the stones, including the foundations. Once the foundation stones are re-laid on their new site on Agilkia the rebuilding of the temple will continue until all the stones are accurately re-sited. The deviation from the old positions is unlikely to be greater than a tenth of an inch, which was the condition laid down for the operation at Abu Simbel, a more difficult situation since the temples had to be cut out of the living rock from which they were originally carved.

Such an undertaking is not without problems. Finance and time are of the utmost importance; anything which slows up the work increases the cost. At present the programme is

running late, due to the lack of power in the early stages for the planned hydraulic filling of the coffer dam. Instead work was started with two groups of excavators and lorries delivering sand to a temporary harbour close to Philae. In this harbour the sand was loaded on to self-dumping barges for transport to the coffer dam, where the cargo was released between the two rows of piles. Recent borings on the proposed coffer-dam line have shown that a change in the line is necessary south of Trajan's Kiosk. This change will result in an increase in the total length of the coffer dam, but it may be possible to use a single row of sheet piles for the modified alignment. If so the available piles would be sufficient for the extra length, but the sand-filling will increase by about 140,000 cubic yards.

Some of the pumps for draining the site have not been used since the High Dam was completed and will require overhaul before draining commences. At first the pumps will be kept near the surface and lowered as the water level falls, and towards the end they will have to be installed in specially dug deep wells. With this type of coffer dam leakage through the sand is likely to be greater in the initial stages before the sand is fully compacted, and as it is extremely difficult to forecast how many pumps will be required to overcome the leakage it is necessary to calculate this on the safe side. In addition a reliable power supply is essential, and although the main supply will come from the High Dam distribution system, diesel generators should be on the spot to stand by for any emergency. Should the pumps fail for any reason during the dismantling of the temples they would once more be covered with muddy water and all the hard work would have to begin again with the attendant difficulty of raising the extra finance. The construction of the coffer dam and the draining of the site are the most important and most difficult of all the work required for the salvaging of the monuments of Philae, but – all being well – the temples should be safely on their new site by the end of 1976, and landscaping, which will cost some £250,000 and require thousands of tons of fertile silt, should be completed in 1977. Like the temples of Abu Simbel the temples of Philae were made to last for eternity. We mortals of this anxious and uncertain age may well wonder if the work of our time is destined to last as long as theirs.

The Philae Obelisk in the decipherment of hieroglyphics

In the great debate concerning the nature of the hieroglyphic script and its decipherment, which took place in the first quarter of the nineteenth century, the monument which occupied the centre of the stage was the Rosetta Stone. From the time of its discovery in 1799, by a French officer serving in the Napoleonic army in Egypt, it was seen as the likely key to the understanding of the writings of ancient Egypt. This supposition was in time proved to be correct. Of the three scripts used to inscribe the texts on the Rosetta Stone, one was Greek and wholly readable. The other two scripts were understood to be ancient Egyptian, one being the formal writing long known from a host of monumental inscriptions, the hiero-glyphic script; the second was cursive, less determinate than hieroglyphic, and was in time termed enchorial, and later demotic, the script 'of the country' or 'of the people'.

The efforts of the early scholars who aimed at solving the problems of the Egyptian scripts were concentrated on making comparisons between the known Greek text and the unknown hieroglyphic and demotic texts, to try to isolate signs or groups of signs which could be confidently paired with Greek words. Several scholars succeeded in proposing equivalences which were ultimately found to be quite correct, but what remained lacking in these small successes was an understanding of the nature of the Egyptian scripts. It was not enough to know that a certain series of signs meant a particular thing; what was needed, initially at least, was an idea of the individual values of the signs, and of how the script 'worked'. Eventually the crucial discoveries were made by the French orientalist Jean-François Champollion, who made his findings known in 1822 in his classic *Lettre à Monsieur Dacier, relative à l'alphabet des hiéroglyphes phonétiques, employés par les Egyptiens pour inscrire sur leurs monuments les titres, les noms et les surnoms des souverains grecs et romains.*

The approach to decipherment was made through the reading of royal names, as the title of Champollion's essay demonstrates. Throughout antiquity the names of Egyptian kings were written in elongated ovals, intended to represent loops of rope, which are now called cartouches. Thomas Young, an English physicist who occupies a notable place among the early workers on hieroglyphic decipherment, was the first to establish beyond reasonable doubt that cartouches contained royal names, and that on the Rosetta Stone the name Ptolemy occurred several times written in cartouche.

At this early juncture in the debate, the Bankes obelisk from 177

Philae played a significant role. The base of the obelisk bore a Greek inscription in which Ptolemy VII Euergetes and his two wives, Cleopatra II and Cleopatra III, were named. At first it was thought by Bankes and by Thomas Young that the hieroglyphic inscription on the obelisk itself was a translation of the Greek text. As two different names were written in cartouches on the obelisk, one of which could be identified with the name Ptolemy as inscribed on the Rosetta Stone, it seemed proper to deduce that the other was Cleopatra. It seems that Bankes may have been the first to suggest this reading, but the proof of the matter was not finally resolved until Champollion demonstrated it conclusively. He succeeded in establishing phonetic values for individual hieroglyphs, and was able to use equivalences in the two names Ptolemy and Cleopatra to clinch his theory. He was also able to show that the text on the obelisk was not the same as the Greek text on the base.

The two cartouches on the Philae obelisk are written as shown to the right.

In the names Ptolemy and Cleopatra, the letters p, t, o, and l are common; three of the hieroglyphs in these cartouches could readily be identified as p (□), o (⚯), and l (⌁); the sign for t in Ptolemy, identified as ⌒, could not be found in its expected position in Cleopatra's name, where ⌖ was found instead. But Champollion, like Thomas Young, was prepared to accept that more than one sign might have the same phonetic value. In dealing with these names the early decipherers were fortunate in that the hieroglyphs of the Graeco-Roman Period were employed much more 'alphabetically' than in earlier periods. It was therefore possible to spell out the royal names on the Philae obelisk with some confidence:

PTOLEMY: □ (P) ⌒ (T) ⚯ (O) ⌁ (L) ⌖ (M) ⫙ (Y) ⎮ (S)
The additional signs in this cartouche represent epithets of the king, 'live for ever' (⚭), and 'beloved of Ptah' (⚳).

CLEOPATRA: △ (K) ⌁ (L) ⎮ (I for E) ⚯ (O) □ (P) ⚘ (A)
⌖ (D for T) ⌖ (R) ⚘ (A)
The final signs ⌒ ◌ represent the Egyptian feminine termination (⌒) and divine determinative (◌).

Champollion's demonstrations of method and his positive discoveries, set out in masterly manner in his famous *Lettre*, were soon recognized as being convincing by most scholars who had interested themselves with the problems of decipherment. But Thomas Young and his supporters, among whom was William Bankes, ever maintained that Champollion based his work very largely on the preliminary discoveries of Young himself. The 178 argument over who should be considered the true and prime decipherer of hieroglyphics persisted throughout the nineteenth century. Today the opinion of most scholars is that Champollion must take the crown; but some still feel that Champollion's triumph is tarnished by his failure to acknowledge the results achieved and published by Young before his own results matured.

Right: The Bankes obelisk at Kingston Lacy.

Abu Simbel ~ Project Completed

Abu Simbel and Philae were the finest monuments to be endangered by the building of the High Dam, and it is a triumph for UNESCO and the countries which supplied money and technical services that Abu Simbel is saved and Philae well on the way to safety. The two temples are very different in character and construction. Abu Simbel, cut out of a sandstone cliff 175 miles south of Philae, is a monument to Ramesses the Great, who lived from 1304 to 1237 B.C. It was a warning to the Nubians and the tribes further south of his absolute power and a glorification of the great man and his deeds. On the other hand Philae, built around 250 B.C., was a religious centre for the worship of the most powerful triad of gods in Ancient Egypt: Osiris, Isis and Horus. The temples and buildings, in contrast with the massive solidity of Abu Simbel, have graceful lines of delicate beauty and float with a pale dream-like quality amongst the rocky outcrops and wild scenery of the territory.

My book *Abu Simbel*, published by Macdonald in 1964, dealt with this monument just before salvage commenced and shows it for the last time in its unique setting in the great cliffs reflected in the sweeping curve of the river. The Egyptian plan which finally found favour was to cut the temples from the living rock in suitably-sized blocks and re-erect them higher up on a safe site.

The first task had to be the construction of a coffer dam to keep out the rising waters of the Nile caused by the building of the High Dam. Like the coffer dam at Philae sheet piling was driven down through the Nile mud until it met bedrock. The dam was 400 yards long and contained 400,000 cubic yards of rock-fill. Pumping stations were installed to overcome seepage. The dam was completed just on time, and at the height of the flood the water came within a few feet of flowing over the crest. Fortunately the work held and the highly skilled and complicated task of extracting the temples from the rock was able to proceed. The first requirement was to remove as quickly as possible the seventy feet of rock above the temples and also the rock which surrounded them on three sides. 330,000 tons of soft sandstone were torn away by huge hook ploughs and the debris used to make roads to the new site. Whilst this was proceeding the interiors of the temples, both walls and ceilings, were buttressed with steel scaffolding, which was padded where it touched the carvings and paintings. When the ploughs had finished their work ample space had been cleared around the temples, which were now only encased in a few feet of rock. Before these were finally cut out block by block, all the cracks and fissures 181 in the sandstone were strengthened by the injection of chemical agents. When these had set the walls and ceilings were reduced to some two feet in thickness by careful hand-sawing before they were cut into blocks for transport. The blocks weighed up to thirty tons apiece and were lifted by steel rods cemented with synthetic resin into deep holes drilled into the stone. Tall derricks placed near the temples lifted the blocks onto low platform trailers where they rested on a bed of soft sand for their journey to the storage area. Each stone was carefully marked and numbered before being moved so that it could easily be found and exactly sited in relation to its fellows during the re-erection. Further protection was provided by strips of adhesive cloth placed along the cut edges and a liberal coating of bonding material was applied to the undersides of the stones.

The first of the 1,050 blocks was cut on 21 May 1965, and on 4 January the following year the first stone was laid on the new site 690 feet from the old one and 200 feet higher up. The coffer dam, now no longer required, was breached and the Nile engulfed the sacred site. The greatest problem of the new location was the construction of artificial cliffs to form an identical setting for the temples. The cliff for the larger temple measured 195 feet in width and 90 feet in height. To carry the enormous weight of rock and to provide anchorage for the façade of the temple it was built in thirty-four arches capable of carrying more than sixty tons to the square yard. The dome formed by the arches stood above the concrete floor from which the ceilings of the tomb chambers were suspended by the original steel lifting rods. The space available enabled adequate ventilation and lighting to be inducted to the temple interiors as well as allowing for the flood-lighting of the exterior. By the autumn of 1966 the temple of Nefertari was completed, followed a year later by the temple of the king. It now only remained to fill in the sixteen miles of joins between the stones, and this was done so expertly that even the closest examination fails to reveal them. An airport and hotel complete with swimming pool set in gardens completed the picture. The temples are identically restored except for their old setting. Twice a year – as for centuries past – the sun's rays enter the inner shrine and illuminate the faces of Ramesses and his three god companions, Ptah, Amen-Re and Re-Harakhty. There is a saying in Ancient Egypt that to speak of the dead is to make them live again. Ramesses the Great is more widely known today than he ever was during his long life.

The Ptolemies

B.C. 304–282 Ptolemy I Soter, Saviour. Son by third wife Berenice I became:

285–246 Ptolemy II Philadelphus, Lover of His Sister. His son by Arsinoe I became:

246–221 Ptolemy III Euergetes, the Benefactor. His son by Berenice II became:

221–205 Ptolemy IV Philopator, Father Lover. His son by Arsinoe III became:

205–180 Ptolemy V Epiphanes, God made Manifest in Living Kings. His son by Cleopatra I became Ptolemy VI and by Cleopatra II Ptolemy VIII.

180–145 Ptolemy VI Philometor, Mother Lover. His son by Cleopatra II became:

145 Ptolemy VII Neos Philopator, New Father Lover. Removed from the throne by the Alexandrians in favour of his younger brother:

145–116 Ptolemy VIII Euergetes II, the Benefactor, also nicknamed Physcon, Fatty. His sons by Cleopatra III became Ptolemies IX and X.

116–107 Ptolemy IX Soter II, Saviour II, nicknamed Lathyros, Chick-pea. Issue Ptolemy XII and Cleopatra IV, who married Ptolemy XI.

107–88 Ptolemy X Alexander I: died in naval battle.

88–81 Ptolemy IX Soter II restored.

80 Ptolemy XI Alexander II. Married Cleopatra IV; was murdered.

80–51 Ptolemy XII Neos Dionysos, the New Dionysus, nicknamed Auletes, Flute Player and Nothos, Bastard. Father of Cleopatra VI and Cleopatra VII by his wife Cleopatra V Tryphaena. Also father of Ptolemies XIII and XIV, mother unknown.

51–30 Cleopatra VII Philopator, Father Lover. She married her half-brothers Ptolemies XIII and XIV. Had a son by Julius Caesar — Caesarion who became:

30 Ptolemy XV Caesarion, who was murdered.

Overlapping dates usually indicate co-regencies.

Chronological Table

Including the names of the principal kings

Early Dynastic Period

First Dynasty (c. 3100–2890 B.C.)	Narmer (Menes) Aha Djer	Den Semerkhet Qaa
Second Dynasty (c. 2890–2686 B.C.)	Hotepsekhemwy Nynetjer	Peribsen Khasekhemwy

Old Kingdom

Third Dynasty (c. 2686–2613 B.C.)	Sanakhte Djoser (Zoser)	Sekhemkhet Huni
Fourth Dynasty (c. 2613–2494 B.C.)	Sneferu Cheops	Chephren Mycerinus
Fifth Dynasty (c. 2494–2345 B.C.)	Userkaf Sahure	Nyuserre Unas
Sixth Dynasty (c. 2345–2181 B.C.)	Teti Pepi I	Merenre Pepi II

First Intermediate Period

A time of political instability lasting from about 2181 B.C. to about 2133 B.C. including the Seventh to Tenth Dynasties, the order and names of whose kings are not fully established.

Middle Kingdom

Eleventh Dynasty (c. 2133–1991 B.C.)	Mentuhotpe I Inyotef I–III	Mentuhotpe II–IV
Twelfth Dynasty (c. 1991–1786 B.C.)	Ammenemes I, 1991–1962 B.C. Sesostris I, 1971–1928 B.C.	Sesostris III, 1878–1843 B.C. Ammenemes III, 1842–1797 B.C.
Thirteenth Dynasty (c. 1786–1633 B.C.)	Sebekhotpe III	Neferhotep

Second Intermediate Period

A further time of political instability during which Egypt was ruled in part by the Asiatic Hyksos. The Fourteenth and Sixteenth Dynasties are particularly shadowy, the former consisting of native rulers, and the latter of minor Hyksos.

Fifteenth (Hyksos) Dynasty (c. 1674–1567 B.C.)	Sheshi Khyan	Apophis I Apophis II
Seventeenth Dynasty (c. 1650–1567 B.C.	Seqenenre	Kamose

New Kingdom

Eighteenth Dynasty (c. 1567–1320 B.C.)	Amosis, 1570–1546 B.C. Amenophis I, 1546–1526 B.C. Tuthmosis I, 1525–1512 B.C. Tuthmosis II, 1512–1504 B.C. Hatshepsut, 1503–1482 B.C. Tuthmosis III, 1504–1450 B.C. Amenophis II, 1450–1425 B.C.	Tuthmosis IV, 1425–1417 B.C. Amenophis III, 1417–1379 B.C. Akhenaten, 1379–1362 B.C. Smenkhkare, 1364–1361 B.C. Tutankhamun, 1361–1352 B.C. Ay, 1352–1348 B.C. Horemheb, 1348–1320 B.C.
Nineteenth Dynasty (c. 1320–1200 B.C.)	Ramesses I, 1320–1318 B.C. Seti I, 1318–1304 B.C. Ramesses II, 1304–1237 B.C.	Merneptah, 1236–1223 B.C. Amenmesses, 1222–1217 B.C. Seti II, 1216–1210 B.C.
Twentieth Dynasty (c. 1200–1085 B.C.)	Sethnakhte, 1200–1198 B.C. Ramesses III, 1198–1166 B.C.	Ramesses IV–XI, 1166–1085 B.C.

Late New Kingdom

From the Twenty-first to the beginning of the Twenty-fifth Dynasties (c. 1085–750 B.C.), Egypt was in political decline. The Twenty-fourth Dynasty was concurrent with the beginning of the Twenty-fifth Dynasty.

Late Period

Twenty-fifth Dynasty (c. 750–656 B.C.)	Piankhi, 750–716 B.C. Shabaka, 716–695 B.C.	Taharqa, 689–664 B.C.
Twenty-sixth Dynasty (c. 664–525 B.C.)	Psammetichus I, 664–610 B.C. Necho II, 610–595 B.C.	Apries, 589–570 B.C. Amasis, 570–526 B.C.

The Twenty-seventh Dynasty consisted of Persian conquering kings, and the Twenty-eighth–Thirtieth Dynasties of the last native Egyptian rulers. In 332 B.C. Alexander the Great conquered Egypt, and thereafter the land was ruled first by Macedonian Greeks (the Ptolemies) and then as part of the Roman Empire.

Twenty-seventh Dynasty (Persian, 525–404 B.C.)	Cambyses, 525–522 B.C. Darius I, 521–486 B.C. Xerxes, 486–466 B.C.	Artaxerxes, 465–424 B.C. Darius II, 424–404 B.C.
Twenty-eighth and Twenty-ninth Dynasties (404–378 B.C.)	Achoris, 393–380 B.C.	
Thirtieth Dynasty (380–343 B.C.)	Nectanebos (Nectanebo I), 380–363 B.C.	Teos, 362–361 B.C. Nectanebos (Nectanebo II), 360–343 B.C.
Macedonian Kings	Alexander the Great, 332–323 B.C. Philip Arrhidaeus, 323–316 B.C. Alexander IV, 316–304 B.C.	

Principal Deities of Ancient Egypt

AMUN (AMEN, AMON): the great god of Thebes of uncertain origin; represented as a man, sometimes ithyphallic; identified with Re as Amen-Re; sacred animals, the ram and the goose.

ANAT: goddess of Syrian origin, with warlike character; represented as a woman holding a shield and an axe.

ANUBIS (ANPU): the jackal-god, patron of embalmers; the great necropolis-god.

ANUKIS (ANQET): goddess of the cataract-region at Aswan; wife of Khnum; represented as a woman with a high feather head-dress.

ARSAPHES (HERISHEF): ram-headed god from Heracleopolis.

ASTARTE: goddess of Syrian origin; introduced into Egypt during the Eighteenth Dynasty.

ATEN: god of the sun-disc, worshipped as the great creator-god by Akhenaten.

ATUM (TUM): the original sun-god of Heliopolis, later identified with Re; represented as a man.

BASTET (BAST): cat-goddess whose cult-centre was at Bubastis in the Delta; in the Late Period regarded as a beneficent deity.

BES: dwarf-deity with leonine features; a domestic god, protector against snakes and various terrors; helper of women in child-birth.

EDJO (WADJET, BUTO): the cobra-goddess of Buto in the Delta; tutelary deity of Lower Egypt, appearing on the royal diadem, protecting the king.

GEB: the earth-god; husband of Nut; member of the Ennead of Heliopolis; represented as a man.

HAPY: god of the Nile in inundation; represented as a man with full, heavy breasts, a clump of papyrus on his head, and bearing heavily laden offering-tables.

HAROERIS: a form of Horus, the 'Elder Horus'; identified with the falcon-god and particularly the patron of the king.

HARPOCRATES (HOR-PA-KHRED): Horus-the-Child, a late form of Horus in his aspect of being son of Isis and Osiris; represented as a naked child wearing the lock of youth and holding one finger to his mouth.

HARSIESIS: a form of Horus, specifically designated 'son of Isis'.

HATHOR: goddess of many functions and attributes; represented often as a cow or a cow-headed woman, or as a woman with horned

AMEN-RE

RE-HARAKHTY

BASTET

HORUS

ISIS

KHNUM

head-dress; the suckler of the king; the 'Golden One'; cult-centres at Memphis, Cusae, Gebelein, Dendera; the patron deity of the mining-region of Sinai; identified by the Greeks with Aphrodite.

HEQET: frog-goddess of Antinoopolis where she was associated with Khnum; a helper of women in child-birth.

HORUS: the falcon-deity, originally the sky-god, identified with the king during his lifetime; also regarded as the son of Osiris and Isis, for the former of whom he became the avenger; cult-centres in many places, e.g. Behdet in the Delta, Hierakonpolis and Edfu in Upper Egypt. See also, Haroeris, Harpocrates, Harsiesis, Re-Harakhty.

IMHOTEP (IMOUTHES): the deified chief minister of Djoser and architect of the Step Pyramid; in the Late Period venerated as the god of learning and medicine; represented as a seated man holding an open papyrus; equated by the Greeks with Asklepios.

ISIS: the divine mother, wife of Osiris and mother of Horus; one of the four 'protector'-goddesses, guarding coffins and Canopic jars; sister of Nephthys with whom she acted as a divine mourner for the dead; in the Late Period Philae was her principal cult-centre.

KHEPRI: the scarab-beetle god, identified with Re as a creator-god; often represented as a beetle within the sun-disc.

KHNUM: ram-headed god of Elephantine, god of the cataract-region; thought to have moulded man on a potter's wheel.

KHONS: the moon-god, represented as a man; with Amun and Mut as a woman with an ostrich-feather on her head.

MAAT: goddess of truth, right, and orderly conduct; represented as a woman with an ostrich-feather on her head.

MIN: the primeval god of Coptos; later revered as a god of fertility, and closely associated with Amun; represented as an ithyphallic human statue, holding a flagellum.

MONTH (MUNT): originally the local deity of Hermonthis, just south of Thebes; later the war-god of the Egyptian king; represented as falcon-headed.

MUT: the divine wife of Amun; cult-centre at Asheru, south of the main temple of Amen-Re at Karnak; originally a vulture-goddess, later represented usually as a woman.

NEFERTUM: the god of the lotus, and hence of unguents; worshipped at Memphis as the son of Ptah and Sakhmet; represented as a man with a lotus-flower head-dress.

NEHEB-KAU: a serpent deity of the underworld, sometimes represented with a man's body and holding the eye of Horus.

NEITH (NET): goddess of Sais; represented as a woman wearing the red crown; her emblem, a shield with crossed arrows; one of the four 'protector'-goddesses who guarded coffins and Canopic jars; identified by the Greeks with Athena.

NEKHBET: vulture-goddess of Nekheb (modern El-Kab); tutelary deity of Upper Egypt, sometimes appearing on the royal diadem beside the cobra (Edjo).

NEPHTHYS (NEBET-HET): sister of Isis; one of the four 'protector'-goddesses, who guarded coffins and Canopic jars; with Isis acted as mourner for Osiris and hence for other dead people; represented as a woman.

NUN (NU): god of the primeval chaos.

NUT: the sky-goddess, wife of Geb, the earth-god; represented as a woman, her naked body curved to form the arch of heaven.

MAAT

OSIRIS (ASAR): the god of the underworld, identified as the dead king; also a god of the inundation and vegetation; represented as a mummified king; principal cult-centre, Abydos.

PTAH: creator-god of Memphis, represented as a man, mummiform, possibly originally as a statue; the patron god of craftsmen; equated by the Greeks with Hephaestus.

PTAH-SEKER-OSIRIS: a composite deity, incorporating the principal gods of creation, death, and after-life; represented like Osiris as a mummified king.

RE (RA): the sun-god of Heliopolis; head of the great Ennead, supreme judge; often linked with other gods aspiring to universality, e.g. Amen-Re, Sobk-Re; represented as falcon-headed; see also Re-Harakhty.

RE-HARAKHTY: a god in the form of a falcon, embodying the characteristics of Re and Horus (here called 'Horus of the Horizon').

SAKHMET: a lion-headed goddess worshipped in the area of Memphis; wife of Ptah; regarded as the bringer of destruction to the enemies of Re.

MIN

SARAPIS: a god introduced into Egypt in the Ptolemaic Period having the characteristics of Egyptian (Osiris) and Greek (Zeus) gods; represented as a bearded man wearing the modius head-dress.

SATIS (SATET): goddess of the island of Siheil in the cataract-region; represented as a woman wearing the white crown with antelope horns; the daughter of Khnum and Anukis.

SELKIS (SELKIT, SERQET): a scorpion-goddess, identified with the scorching heat of the sun; one of the four 'protector'-goddesses, guarding coffins and Canopic jars; shown sometimes as a woman with a scorpion on her head.

SESHAT: the goddess of writing; the divine keeper of royal annals; represented as a woman.

SETH (SET, SUTEKH): the god of storms and violence; identified with many animals, including the pig, ass, okapi, and hippopotamus;

188 represented as an animal of unidentified type; brother of Osiris

OSIRIS

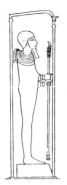

PTAH

and his murderer; the rival of Horus; equated by the Greeks with Typhon.

SHU: the god of air; with Tfenet, forming the first pair of gods in the Heliopolitan ennead; shown often as a man separating Nut (sky) from Geb (earth).

SOBK (SEBEK, SUCHOS): the crocodile-god, worshipped throughout Egypt, but especially in the Faiyum, and at Gebelein and Kom Ombo in Upper Egypt.

TFENET: the goddess of moisture; with Shu forming the first pair of the Heliopolitan ennead.

THOERIS (TAURT, TAWERET): the hippopotamus-goddess; a beneficent deity, the patron of women in child-birth.

THOTH: the ibis-headed god of Hermopolis; the scribe of the gods and the inventor of writing, the ape as well as the ibis being sacred to him.

UNNEFER (WENEN-NEFER, ONNOPHRIS): a name meaning 'he who is continually happy', given to Osiris after his resurrection.

SETH

THOTH

SHU SUPPORTING NUT

Further Reading

H. I. BELL, *Egypt from Alexander the Great to the Arab Conquest*. Oxford, 1948.

E. R. BEVAN, *A History of Egypt under the Ptolemaic Dynasty*. London, 1927.

J. ČERNÝ, *Ancient Egyptian Religion*. London, 1952.

A. B. EDWARDS, *A Thousand Miles up the Nile*. London, 1877

P. M. FRASER, *Ptolemaic Alexandria*. 3 vols. Oxford, 1972.

A. H. GARDINER, *Egypt of the Pharaohs*. Oxford, 1961.

MICHAEL GRANT, *Cleopatra*. London, 1972.

ERIK IVERSEN, *Obelisks in Exile*. II, *The Obelisks of Istanbul and England*. Copenhagen, 1972.

H. KEES, *Ancient Egypt. A Cultural Topography*. London, 1961.

WILLIAM MACQUITTY, *Abu Simbel*. London, 1965.

SIEGFRIED MORENZ, *Egyptian Religion*. London, 1973.

G. POSENER (ed.), *A Dictionary of Egyptian Civilization*. London, 1962.

A. E. P. WEIGALL, *A Guide to the Antiquities of Upper Egypt*. London, 1910.

R. E. WITT, *Isis in the Graeco–Roman World*. London, 1971.

A General Introductory Guide to the Egyptian Collections in the British Museum. London, 1964.

Index

ABU SIMBEL, 9, 25, 56, 77, 92, 156, 158, 160, 163, 165, 169, 173, 176, 181–2
Abydos, 37, 40, 82
Actium, 117
Agilkia, 8, 119, 159, 168, 173
Akasha, 24
Akhenaten, 36, 54, 69
Alexander the Great, King, 72, 86, 91–2, 94, 96
Alexander II, King, 94
Alexandria, 59, 86, 88, 92, 94, 95, 104, 109, 113, 117, 118
Amemit, 60
Amenhotep III, King, 36
Amenuphis III, King, 144
Amen-Re, 25, 36, 72, 77, 144, 181
Amun, 22, 36, 83, 92, 145, 152
Anat cult, 85
Antiochus the Great, 96
Antiochus IV, 100
Antoninus Pius, 32, 150
Antony, Mark, 32, 86, 104, 113, 114, 115, 117–18
Anubis, 36, 55, 60, 83, 150
Anukis, 123, 129
Aphrodite, 105, 114
Arsenuphis, 96, 129
Arsinoe I, 95
Arsinoe II, 95
Arsinoe III, 96
Arsinoe IV, 104–5, 115
Arundale, Francis, 46, 141
Astarte cult, 85
Aswan, 24, 28, 30, 32, 34, 40, 45, 58, 120, 122, 123, 137
Aswan Dam: first High, 7–8, 23, 25, 28, 119, 127, 141, 155, 157; second, 156–76, 181
Atbara, 22
Atum, 49
Augustus, 25, 129, 153
Auletes, 105, 108, 109
Awad, 119

BABYLON, 92, 95
Bankes, Ralph, 48, 133
Bankes, William John, 133, 136–7, 141, 144, 177–9
Beit el-Wali, 22
Belzoni, Giovanni, 136–7
Berenice IV, 101, 104, 105
Bes, 70, 85, 153
Biban el-Moluk, 69
Bigeh, 1, 83, 119, 122, 129, 152, 153, 160
Blue Nile, 17, 18–19, 166–7
Book of the Dead, 65, 68, 86
Bruce, James, 17
Bubastis, 56
Buddha, 59, 86, 87
Buhen, 25

Buto, 55, 66, 94, 104
Byblos, 55

CAESAR, Julius, 32, 36, 86, 91, 104, 109, 112–13, 114
Caesarion, 36–7, 91, 113, 114, 117–18
Cairo, 40, 88, 136–7
Caligula, 25
Caracalla, 32
Carter, Howard, 72
Cerny, Professor, 80
Champollion, Jean-François, 48, 177–9
Cheops, 68–9, 159
Churchill, Sir Winston, 155
Claudius, 32, 153
Cleopatra I, 100
Cleopatra II, 100, 147, 178
Cleopatra III, 100, 129, 178
Cleopatra V, 105
Cleopatra VI, 104
Cleopatra VII, 32, 36–7, 91, 100–1, 104, 105, 108, 109, 112, 114–18, 153
Cleopatra's Needle, 48
Commodus, 32
Constantine the Great, 88
Copts, 79, 88, 90, 141
Cornelius Gallus, 153
Crassus, 109
Curzon, Robert, 150, 152

DARIUS, 92
Debod, 25
Decius, 32
Deir el-Bahri, 76, 144
Deir el-Medina, 29
Delgo, 24
Dendera, 29, 32, 36–7, 46, 70, 80, 95, 104, 112, 114, 117, 144
Dendur, 25
Desaix, General, 141
Diodorus, 77
Dionysus, 105, 114
Djoser, 53, 68, 126, 159
Domitian, 32, 115
Drovetti, Bernardino, 136–7, 141, 144
Duamutef, 58

EDFU, 29, 30, 32, 36, 37, 95, 104, 141
Edwards, Amelia B., 8, 23, 25, 27, 123, 147–8, 154
Egypt Exploration Society, 8, 53
El-Amarna, 54
El-Badari, 16
El Hasa, 119
El-Qurna, 29
Elephantine, 25, 28, 40, 119, 122–4, 127, 147
Emery, Professor Bryan, 53
Ennead, 49
Ergamenes, 101
Esna, 29, 32, 42, 45, 95

Euphrates, 13

FAIYUM, 16

GANDHARA, 59
Gardiner, Sir Alan, 54
Geb, 49
Gebel Adda, 165, 173
Gemmai, 24
George IV, 137
Geta, 32
Giza, Great Pyramids at, 17, 68–9, 120–1
Grant, Lt.-Col. J. A., 17
Gregory XVI, Pope, 149

HADRIAN, 32, 88, 152
Hanna, Dr W. S., 168
Hapi, 50, 58, 153
Harendotes, 153
Harpocrates, 72, 79, 141
Harsiesis, 129, 150, 152
Hathor, 7, 28, 32, 36, 46, 60, 72, 79, 86, 96, 100, 101, 105, 115, 128, 137, 141, 145, 147, 152, 153, 155
Hatshepsut, 76, 144
Heket, 150
Hermes Trismegistus, 115
Hermopolis, 127
Herodotus, 13, 17
High Dam Authority, 168
Homer, 96
Horsmataui, 37
Horus, 25, 30, 32, 36, 37, 40, 54, 55–6, 59, 79, 83, 85, 86, 90, 96, 101, 105, 108, 109, 113, 115, 128, 129, 133, 141, 144, 145, 147, 152, 153, 181
Horus Behudet, 37

IHY, 46
Imhotep, 53, 68
Imsety, 58
Io, 115
Isis, goddess of Philae, 25, 28, 37, 40, 49, 50, 54, 55–6, 58, 59, 70, 79, 83, 85, 86, 87, 88, 90, 96, 101, 105, 108, 109, 113, 115, 128, 129, 133, 141, 145, 147, 150, 152, 153, 181
Issus, 92

JESUS, 87
Justinian, 149

KADRI, Ahmed, 168
Kagemni, 19
Kalabsha, 25, 32, 34, 57
Karnak, 29, 30, 32, 36, 42, 83
Kerma, 23
Kertassi, 25
Khartoum, 17–18, 19, 22
Khnum, 32, 42, 57, 123, 127, 129

Khons, *28, 100*
Kom Ombo, *13, 14–15, 28–9, 30, 37,
    60, 66, 82, 100, 104, 105, 108, 113*
Khrushchev, Nikita, *157*
Ksar Anas el-Wogud, *119*
Kumma, *24*
Kwan-Yin, *59*

LAKE ALBERT, *17*
Lake Nasser, *162, 166–7*
Lake Tana, *18, 22*
Leptis Magna, *137*
Lucius Antonius, *117*
Luxor, *8, 16, 29, 30, 32, 36, 48, 50, 58,
    72, 83, 144*
Lyon, Captain Henry, *155*

MAET, *56*
Mahatta, *23*
Maheu, René, *168*
Mandulis, *25*
Marcus Aurelius, *32, 113, 152*
Mataria, *88*
Medinet Habu, *29, 72, 76, 85*
Memphis, *27, 45, 83, 86, 90*
Menes, *91*
Meroe, *22*
Min, *72, 82*
Mohammed Ali, *133, 136*
Montu, *36*
Moses, *115*
Moukhtar, Dr Gamal, *168*
Mufumbiro mountains, *17*
Murad Bey, *141*
Mut, *83, 145*
Mycerinus, *120*

NAKHT, *66*
Napata, *22*
Nasser, President Gamal Abdel, *156*
Nebamun, *8, 16*
Nectanebos I, *36, 87, 122, 141, 144*
Nectanebos II, *128–9*
Neferkare, Pepi II, *123–4*
Nefertari, *50, 182*
Nefertiti, *54*
Neith, *58*
Nekhbet, *66, 94, 104, 144, 150*
Nephthys, *49, 50, 58, 129, 141, 147,
    150, 152, 153*
Nero, Emperor, *17*
Nile, river, *1, 9, 13, 16, 24–5, 40–1, 50,
    52, 55, 58, 59, 83, 92, 96, 112, 119,
    122, 124–7, 142–3, 153, 154, 155, 157,
    158, 160, 163, 168, 169, 181*: First
    Cataract, *25, 27–8, 119, 120, 123,
    125, 150*; Second Cataract, *8, 24, 25,
    125*; Third Cataract, *23, 24*; Fourth
    Cataract, *22*; Fifth Cataract, *22*;
    Sixth Cataract, *22*; Lower, *91*;
    Upper, *91*
Nun, *50*
Nubia, *7, 17, 23, 25, 28–9, 120, 123,
    153, 168–9, 181*
Nut, *49*

OCTAVIAN, *113, 114, 117–18*
Olympias, *91*
Osiris, *25, 36, 37, 40, 45, 49, 54, 55–6,
    58, 60, 70, 82, 83, 85–6, 90, 105,
    108, 114, 115, 129, 144, 145, 147,
    149–50, 152, 181*

Ozymandias, *77*

PAUL of Tarsus, *87*
Pelusium, *109*
Penebtaui, *28*
Pepi I, *123*
Pharsalia, *109*
Philae: island of, *17, 22, 25, 40, 49, 83,
    87, 88, 90, 119–54*; temple of, *8–9,
    12, 13, 28–9, 36, 54, 77, 79, 91, 94,
    95, 96, 181*; first Great Pylon, *7, 96,
    104, 110, 122, 127, 128, 129, 132,
    133, 134–5, 141, 144, 150*; temple to
    Imhotep, *96, 129*; second Great
    Pylon, *105, 122, 134–5, 145–7, 152,
    153*; Birth House, *122, 133, 134–7,
    144*; kiosk of Trajan, *122, 139–40,
    153, 154*; temple of Harendotes, *122,
    153*; Outer Court, *127, 129, 141*;
    East Colonnade, *129*; Gate of
    Ptolemy II, *129*; Quay Wall, *129*;
    temple of Arsenuphis, *129*; Vestibule
    of Nectanebos, *129*; sanctuary of
    Isis, *130–1, 144, 147*; boat of Isis,
    149; Osiris chambers, *149–50*;
    Hadrian's gateway, *153, 154*; temple
    of Augustus, *153*; temple of Hathor,
    153
Philip II, *91–2*
Philip V, *96*
Pinturiccio, *115*
Plutarch, *114*
Pompey, *109, 113*
Ptolemy I, Soter, *85, 92, 94, 95*
Ptolemy II, Philadelphus, *91, 92, 95,
    141*
Ptolemy III, Euergetes I, *28, 30, 32, 36
    91, 95, 141, 149*
Ptolemy IV, Philopator, *28, 30, 36, 96,
    101*
Ptolemy V, Epiphanes, *28, 96, 100,
    101, 129*
Ptolemy VI, Philometor, *28, 32, 79,
    100, 129, 144, 145, 153*
Ptolemy VII, Neos Philopator, *100, 108*
Ptolemy VIII, Euergetes II, *28–9, 30,
    36, 72, 79, 100, 104, 105, 129, 144,
    147, 153, 178*
Ptolemy IX, Soter *11, 100, 104, 105*
Ptolemy X, Alexander I, *101, 144*
Ptolemy XI, *101*
Ptolemy XII, Neos Dionysos, *29, 32,
    36, 96, 104, 105, 128, 141, 144, 145,
    147*
Ptolemy XIII, *105, 108, 109, 112*
Ptolemy XIV, *105, 112, 113–14*
Ptolemy XV, *113, 114, 117*
Ptah, *77, 182*

QADESH, cult, *85*
Qebhsenuef, *58*
Quebet el Hawa, *24*

RAMESSES the Great, *27, 48, 77, 156,
    181–2*
Ramesses II, *22, 40*
Ramesses III, *76, 82, 85*
Ramesses VI, *36–7, 72, 80*
Ramesseum, the, *29, 48, 77*
Re, *50, 55, 85, 127*
Re-Harakhty, *56, 77, 158, 182*

Rosetta Stone, *40, 177–8*
Rostem, Osman, *161*

SAAD-EL-AALI, *157, 159*
Sabu, *24*
Sakhmet, *85*
Salt, Henry, *133, 136, 144*
Saqqara, *18, 19, 53, 54, 68*
Sarapis, *85, 86, 88*
Satis, *123, 129*
Seleucids, *96, 100*
Selkis, *58*
Semna, *24*
Senedjem, *58*
Sennar, *19*
Sennuphis, *113*
Seth, *36, 49, 55, 153*
Seti I, *40, 64*
Severus, *32*
Shelfak, *24*
Shelley, Percy Bysshe, *77*
Shendi, *22*
Shu, *49, 150*
Siheil, island of, *28, 32, 119, 126*
Silsila, *28, 29*
Smithsonian Institute, *165, 173*
Sobk, *28, 60, 100*
Sostratus, *96*
Speke, John Hanning, *17*
Step Pyramid, *68–9, 126*
Sudd, *18*
Sulb, *24*
Sulla, *101*

TAFA, *25*
Taharqa, *22, 128, 145*
Tanis, *45, 48*
Tarsus, *114, 115*
Tasent-Nofret, *28*
Tfenet, *49, 129*
Thebes, *32, 36, 54, 77, 83, 101*
Theodorus, Bishop, *147, 149*
Theodosius the Great, *90*
Theodotus, *108, 109*
Thoeris, *85*
Thoth, *53, 60, 85, 127, 144*
Thrace, *97*
Thutmosis III, *48*
Tiberius, *129, 144, 152*
Tisiat Falls, *18*
Trajan, *25, 32, 122, 153*
Tutankhamun, *9, 25, 36–7, 58, 64, 72,
    165*

UMAR, *90*
UNESCO, *9, 25, 165, 168, 181*
Unnefer, *129, 141*
Uronarti, *24*

WADI HALFA, *25*
Wazet, *144*
Weigall, A. E. P., *30*
Wellington, Duke of, *137*
Wells, H. G., *88*
White Nile, *17, 18–19*
Witt, R. E., *115*

YOUNG, Thomas, *177–9*

ZEUS, *85*